Living
Our
Beliefs

by
Kenneth L. Carder

Reprinted 1998

EDITOR'S NOTE: Quotations from the writings of John Wesley and others have been left in their original form. John Wesley and others quoted wrote and lived in an era when gender-inclusive language was neither norm nor practice.

Library of Congress Catalog Card No. 96-84123

ISBN 0-88177-169-4

DR169

Contents

Preface

Christian doctrine serves a special function in the United Methodist tradition. Beliefs, in the Wesleyan heritage, function primarily in the service of character formation, faith development, missional engagement, and evangelization. Wesley's emphasis on practical divinity prevented doctrines and beliefs from becoming primarily theoretical speculations, academic pursuits, or legal evidence against heretics. Wesley's preoccupation with the way to salvation caused him to evaluate doctrines in terms of their impact on living. His primary concern was the relationship between beliefs and behavior, doctrine and discipleship, theological concepts and Christian character. In other words, *beliefs* are to be lived; *doctrine* is to be practiced. *That is the United Methodist way.*

United Methodist beliefs are shared by most other Christian denominations. United Methodism likely is recognized more for its polity than for its doctrinal distinctiveness. Since both the Catholic/Anglican and the Reformed theological traditions converge in The United Methodist Church, the church encompasses a breadth of doctrinal and theological perspectives and emphases. The United Methodist Church, however, is committed to maintaining doctrinal standards while interpreting and applying the historic doctrines in the contemporary contexts.

United Methodist doctrine and beliefs are means of *holy living,* not guidelines for identifying heretics. The primary purpose of beliefs is evangelization and the formation of Christian disciples, not determining who is inside the acceptable parameters of orthodoxy. The authenticity of beliefs lies in their ability to shape persons and communities into the image of Christ and promote holiness and happiness. Do they promote love for God and neighbor? That is an important Wesleyan test of doctrines and beliefs.

Utilizing Wesley's sermons, the approved doctrinal/theological statement in *The United Methodist Book of Discipline (1992)*, the liturgical resources in *The United Methodist Hymnal*, and other materials, this book attempts to identify United Methodist beliefs and their relevance for living as disciples of Jesus Christ. Laity and clergy are encouraged to use the book as a resource for living their beliefs, which is the United Methodist way.

The book originated in response to an invitation from David Hazlewood and the staff of Discipleship Resources. David and his colleagues recognized a need for a resource to be used by laity and clergy in identifying and living United Methodist beliefs. Being asked to write such a resource is a distinct honor, and with honor always comes responsibility. David and his co-workers have provided invaluable support in enabling me to fulfill the responsibility. Debra Ball-Kilbourne's editorial contribution has been especially insightful and helpful.

I am indebted to the Wesley Seminary faculty, particularly James C. Logan, Bobby McLean, M. Douglas Meeks, Ted Campbell, Kendall Soulen, Lawrence Stookey, David Lowes Watson, and Sondra Wheeler. The roundtable discussions with them forced me to probe more deeply and opened avenues of new understanding. Written critiques by Jim Logan, David Watson, and Kendall Soulen (of an early manuscript) raised important issues and precipitated additional study and reflection on my part. Although these scholars cannot be faulted for the flaws in the book, they contributed enormously to my own understanding and appreciation of our Wesleyan theological tradition and challenge.

Toward the end of his long years of living and proclaiming his beliefs, John Wesley reflected upon the future of the Methodist movement. By all statistical measurements, the movement was strong and continuing to grow throughout Europe and America. Yet Wesley was disturbed by the apparent weakening of Methodist moral influence, evangelical commitment, and missional involvement. He wrote in 1786:

I am not afraid that the people called Methodists should ever cease to exist either in Europe or America. But I am afraid lest they should only exist as a dead sect, having the form of religion without the power. And this undoubtedly will be the case unless they hold fast both the doctrine, spirit, and discipline with which they first set out.[1]

Contemporary Methodists must seek to live the doctrine, discipline, and spirit with which the movement began. *That is the United Methodist way!*

Chapter One

Why a United Methodist?

Richard Allen, the founder of the African Methodist Episcopal Church, was born into slavery on February 14, 1760. At the age of seventeen, he was converted by the preaching of Freeborn Garrettson and joined the Methodist Society. He was licensed to preach in 1782. One of two black preachers at the organizing conference of the Methodist Episcopal Church in 1784, he became a member of the Old St. George's Methodist Society in Philadelphia. While praying at St. George's in 1794, he and a few black colleagues were literally pulled from their knees by an official of the Society. Allen and his friends left St. George's and subsequently formed the AME Church.

Although he was cruelly mistreated by some white Methodists, Richard Allen wrote, "I feel thankful that ever I heard a Methodist preach. We are beholden to the Methodists, under God, for the light of the Gospel we enjoy."[1] He was asked to be the pastor of a non-Methodist African Church in Philadelphia. He offered the following as his reason for refusing the position: "I told them I could not accept their offer, as I was a Methodist . . . I informed them that I could not be anything else but a Methodist . . ."[2]

Waning Denominational Loyalty

Few United Methodists today consider that they "could not be anything else but a Methodist." Church loyalty is related less to denominational labels and historic roots than programs offered, convenience of location, and family and friendship ties. Denominationalism, as has been known and practiced in the United States during the last two hundred years, may be coming to an end. It is not uncommon for persons to be members of several different denominations in their lifetimes. The differences *among denominations* seem less significant than the differences among congregations *within the same denomination.*

Denominational identity no longer has the appeal it once enjoyed. Preachers could, a few decades ago, attract a following through denominational chauvinism. Churches could be built by condemning other churches and extolling the superiority of one's own denomination. Such a message today receives but isolated positive response. Most preachers now are far more critical of their own denomination than other communions.

At the same time that denominational loyalty has been waning, many denominations are attempting to rediscover their doctrinal identity. Methodism, for example, has experienced an enormous increase in Wesleyan scholarship during the last twenty years. Similar research is taking place in other traditions. Are the trends toward less denominational loyalty and more interest in theological or doctrinal identity contradictory and mutually exclusive? If denominational loyalty is waning, why bother with learning the historic doctrines and beliefs of particular traditions? Why be concerned about what Methodists believe? Why not simply focus on what Christians believe and ignore the distinctiveness of denominations? *After all, is not what we share in common far more significant than our differences?*

Nourished by Common Roots

These are important questions which merit response. First, our primary loyalty must be to Jesus Christ and the Christian gospel. *We are Christians first.* Reception into membership of a United Methodist Church is first and foremost membership in the church universal. Baptized members of other denominations are received into membership in The United Methodist Church without being re-baptized. Professions of faith made in other denominational contexts are considered valid. Since United Methodism is not a "confessional" church with one creed to which members are asked to subscribe, membership preparation tends to give less emphasis to distinctive United Methodist doctrinal positions.

The doctrinal/theological statement in *The Book of Discipline*[3] identifies the following as basic Christian affirmations that we share in common with other communions:

- We confess belief in the triune God—Father, Son and Holy Spirit.
- We hold a faith in the mystery of salvation in and through Jesus Christ.
- God's redemptive love is realized in human life by the activity of the Holy Spirit, both in personal experience and in the community of believers.
- We are part of Christ's universal church when by adoration, proclamation, and service we become conformed to Christ.
- The reign of God is both a present and future reality.
- Scripture is authoritative in matters of faith.
- Our justification as sinners is by grace through faith.
- The church is in need of continual reformation and renewal.
- The essential oneness of the church in Jesus Christ is affirmed in the historic creeds.

Methodism's doctrinal/theological foundation, therefore, has more to do with *emphases* than with *distinctiveness*. Methodism's theological identity has been formed by certain emphases within the church universal. *The Book of Discipline* states: "Nourished by common roots of this shared Christian heritage, the branches of Christ's Church have developed diverse traditions that enlarge our store of shared understandings. Our avowed ecumenical commitment as United Methodists is to gather our own doctrinal emphases into the larger Christian unity, there to be made more meaningful in a richer whole."[4]

Just as we all share in a common humanity but are enriched by distinctive heritages and traits, Christians share in common primary commitment to Jesus Christ and are made richer by particular faith stories and emphases. Our officially approved position affirms: "If we are to offer our best gifts to the common Christian treasury, we must make a deliberate effort as a church to strive for critical self-understanding. It is as Christians involved in ecumenical partnership that we embrace and examine our distinctive heritage."[5]

A Movement of Mission and Reform

Methodism began as a mission and reform movement within the Church of England. Methodism did not arise in response to doctrinal controversy. The leaders did not set out to reformulate doctrine but to summon people to experience and live the grace of God and to grow in their knowledge and love of God. John Wesley said that God had raised up the Methodists to "reform the nation, particularly the Church, and to spread scriptural holiness over the land."[6] Reform and mission grew out of the early Methodists' experience and understanding of God. Doctrinal interpretation, evangelical proclamation, discipleship formation, and social witness were considered to be inseparable components of a vital relationship with God. The results included a spiritual and moral revival in England and America.

The conditions existing in England in the 1700s are parallel to those confronting us at the dawning of the twenty-first century. The Enlightenment and the emerging scientific revolution offered alternative views of the world and new means of dealing with personal and societal problems. The industrial revolution intensified the economic disparity between the rich and the poor and brought a new wave of exploitation. The poor were depersonalized. Children were at risk as they labored in the factories and mines. Slavery was a thriving business and existed with minimal protest from the established religious institutions. Suffering and death stalked the human family. Medical care was beyond the reach of the masses. Hedonism increased as the strict morality of Victorian England gave way to moral relativity, freedom, and uncertainty. The established church lost its appeal to the masses, particularly the poor. Its moral and ethical influence was minimal. Crime and violence threatened society. Prisons and the gallows were prevalent methods of dealing with the rising crime rate. The nation seemed to have lost its spiritual and moral compass and moorings.

In Need of Revival

The contemporary world stands in need of spiritual and moral revival. We are confronted with the inadequacy of old answers to familiar questions and uncertain answers to new questions. Our society has become increasingly secularized; religion has been marginalized in the public consciousness and institutions. Exalting the scientific method as the supreme path to truth has rendered divine revelation suspect. The promotion of individual freedom, self-expression and self-fulfillment above community responsibility and solidarity has undermined civic accountability and love of neighbor. Morality and ethics have been relativized and left to personal preferences, resulting in moral uncertainty at best and moral anarchy at worst. The disparity between the rich and the poor grows and millions of people are dying from lack of life's basic necessities. Violence and crime stalk our neighborhoods. Longer prison sentences and the death penalty have again become the primary solutions offered for the problems of crime and violence. Mainline churches are declining in membership and influence. They seldom include the impoverished masses in their membership. A deep spiritual void exists into which destructive forces are moving.

In spite of phenomenal scientific and technological advances and economic growth, unparalleled suffering plagues the human family. While many diseases—which once meant certain death—have been removed, new diseases now threaten entire populations. Science and technology have increased the speed and expanse of transportation and communication; they have also created weapons which killed more people in the twentieth century than in all previous centuries combined. Economic wealth has greatly increased, yet more people are dying of poverty related causes than ever in history. Even though the exploitation of children is denounced by most nations, approximately ten to twenty million children die each year from poverty. More children than soldiers now die from war. In a century in which human rights came to the forefront of concern, we persecute and slaughter millions of people because of race, gender, religion, and national origin. The twentieth century has been both an age of progress and an age of agony. *Without a spiritual*

*and moral revival, the suffering is likely to encompass even more
of us in the twenty-first century.*

Plain Doctrine . . . Good Discipline

A recovery of the theological emphases, which sparked the
Wesleyan revival in the eighteenth century, has the potential of
igniting a revival as we enter the twenty-first century. Spiritual
renewal comes as a gift of God. It does not result from new programs or structures offered by the church. Efforts to revitalize
the church through strategic planning processes and programmat-
ic emphases are destined to fail. Only by sharing in God's life
and mission through the power of the Holy Spirit does renewal
take place. Without that vital sharing in the presence, purposes,
and action of God, all strategies and structures are but pious
idols and improved means to unimproved ends. The traditional
Methodist summons to "experience the justifying and sanctifying
grace of God and encourage people to grow in the knowledge
and love of God through the personal and corporate disciplines
of the Christian life"[7] remains our primary challenge.

Richard Allen's reason for being a Methodist had nothing to
do with denominational superiority or doctrinal uniqueness. He
attributed the Methodists' effectiveness in awakening and con-
verting people to the gospel to "plain doctrine and . . . good discipline."[8] His concern far exceeded institutional chauvinism.
Allen was convinced that Methodism offered a doorway into the
life of God and a means of sharing in Christ's ministry to the
world.

Efforts to clarify the beliefs of United Methodists are not
directed toward creating denominational pride or setting The
United Methodist Church apart from other churches. *The goal is
to use the Wesleyan tradition as a doorway into knowledge and
love of God.* As a branch is nourished through its roots,
Methodism's doctrinal and theological roots are means by which
God can nourish us with divine grace and graft us into Christ's
mission in the world.

*The transformation of the world is God's preoccupation, not
the statistical growth of the institutional church.* The church is
only an instrument of God's mission—called to be a sign, fore-

taste, and vehicle of God's new heaven and new earth. Its identity is in its relationship with God and its involvement in Christ's ministry of reconciliation in a broken, suffering, and sinful world. It must, therefore, ask anew the basic questions: Who is the God known in Jesus Christ? What is God doing in the world? What is the appropriate response to the nature and action of God?

Opportunities for Reflection

The following questions may be used by groups wishing to discuss the material in Chapter One or by individuals wanting to reflect on issues raised within the chapter.

1. Richard Allen believed he could only be a Methodist. How important is denominational loyalty to you? Why are you a part of The United Methodist Church?

2. What parallels do you find between England in the 1800s and your twenty-first century experience? How might these similarities affect The United Methodist Church? Your local congregation?

Chapter Two

God Verses Idols

Beliefs Matter

"It makes no difference what you believe as long as you are sincere." Such an affirmation of faith has been widely espoused in the name of faith and tolerance. The affirmation, which is itself a belief, makes sincerity the criteria for authentic faith. It assumes that all religious beliefs are equal and their validity is judged by the firmness with which they are held and the sincerity with which they are acted upon. Truth becomes synonymous with strong conviction, and faithfulness is validated by "it feels right."

In a world of conflicting ideas, multiple faith options, and competing loyalties, the minimizing of the importance of religious beliefs has its appeal. Tough thinking and potentially divisive discernment become unnecessary. Furthermore, science and technology seemingly have rendered many religious concepts irrelevant. No longer do we depend upon religion to explain the world. Science provides answers to questions once considered the domain of religion. Technology, economics, medicine, and politics provide solutions to problems once relegated to religious faith. In a world which defines truth as verifiable facts, religious beliefs seem to be merely speculative. As speculations and conjectures, they are held tentatively, awaiting empirical verification; or they are placed in a pious compartment of the mind isolated from the decisions and actions of everyday life. The religious beliefs themselves cease to matter. Only sincerity matters.

Indifferent to Doctrine?

A perception persists that "one can believe anything and be United Methodist." Such a characterization has deep roots in our history. Methodism began as a movement within the Church of England. Wesley and the early Methodists were occupied with evangelization and mission more than with the formulation of systematic doctrines. Wesley and his colleagues *presumed* and *affirmed* the basic doctrines and beliefs of the church of which they were part. The Articles of Religion, the Book of Common Prayer, and the Homilies of the Anglican Church formed the foundation of Methodist beliefs. Although he held tenaciously to the historic doctrines of the Christian faith and taught them to others, Wesley's emphasis was upon evangelization and the pursuit of "holiness of heart and life." That emphasis continued in America when the Methodists formed the Methodist Episcopal Church in 1784. The Articles of Religion of the Anglican Church and the Heidelberg Catechism of the Reformed tradition form the bedrock of belief of the churches which formed into The United Methodist Church. Yet the emphasis in all of the Methodist traditions has been on evangelization and holy living more than doctrinal refinement and creedal confession.

Adding to the perception that Methodists are indifferent to doctrine is the emphasis upon pluralism and diversity. Wesley's commitment to "catholic spirit," or the oneness of the church in Jesus Christ, has often been misinterpreted to mean an indulgent indifference that makes sound doctrine subservient to tolerance. Further, Methodism's historic openness to diversity, its insistence on freedom 'to think and let think', and the belief that continuing exploration into the nature and purposes of God is a necessary component of faith have led some to assume that no doctrinal parameters exist. As *The Book of Discipline* states: "Wesley's familiar dictum was: 'As to all opinions which do not strike at the root of Christianity, we think and let think.'"[1] However, although Wesley and the Methodists "were fully committed to the principles of religious toleration and theological diversity they were equally confident that there is a 'marrow' of Christian truth that can be identified and that must be conserved."[2]

Beliefs Affect Living

The notion that Methodists are indifferent to doctrine is a gross misrepresentation of our heritage and identity. Methodists take religious belief with the utmost seriousness. We know that beliefs shape behavior and practice. Beliefs and the stories that express them influence our self-image, our relationships, and our commitments. *The Book of Discipline* states: "No motif in the Wesleyan tradition has been more constant than the link between Christian doctrine and Christian living."[3] Wesley considered beliefs and doctrines primarily in terms of their significance for Christian discipleship. He was not interested in religious ideas divorced from living. Because beliefs affect living, Methodists are deeply concerned about doctrines.

Beliefs shape our self-image, our view of our own worth and destiny. It matters whether we consider ourselves worthless creatures or children of God, unredeemed sinners or forgiven disciples, hopeless victims of sin and death or citizens of an eternal kingdom. Beliefs affect our relationships with others. It matters whether other people are believed to be enemies or brothers and sisters, inferior means to our ends or persons made in God's image and redeemed in Jesus Christ, sinners deserving of our retribution or sinners in need of love. Beliefs influence our relationship with the world. It matters whether we see creation as a commodity over which we have ownership or as "our Father's world" in which we are tillers, nurturers, and stewards. Beliefs fashion our relationship with God. It matters whether we believe God is a cruel judge or a loving parent, an impersonal force or a personal friend, one who rules by coercive power and fear or one whose power is love. It matters if God is detached from the world and human experience or if God is present with the world and invites human beings to share in the divine life.

Practical Divinity

Another factor that may help explain the perception that

beliefs are secondary to Methodists is the Wesleyan emphasis on
"practical divinity." Wesley's primary concern was holy living
characterized by loving God and one's neighbor with Christlike
love. He wrote:

> *I believe the merciful God regards the lives and*
> *tempers of men more than their ideas. I believe*
> *he respects the goodness of the heart rather than*
> *the clearness of the head; and that if the heart of*
> *a man be filled (by the grace of God, and the*
> *power of his Spirit) with the humble, gentle,*
> *patient love of God and man, God will not cast*
> *him into everlasting fire prepared for the devil*
> *and his angels because his ideas are not clear,*
> *or because his conceptions are confused.*
> *Without holiness, I own, no man shall see the*
> *Lord; but I dare not add, or clear ideas.*[4]

The Methodist view of the primacy of holy living, however,
is itself a significant belief. It is rooted in confidence in God's
grace which has the power to make us holy. It also results from
the understanding of faith as acting upon the promises of God.
Wesley knew from personal experience and observation that people *act their way into believing* as well as *believe their way into
acting.* Peter Böhler's advice to Wesley rang true to his subsequent experience, "Preach faith *till* you have it, and then,
because you have it, you *will* preach faith."[5] The Methodist
emphasis upon "practical divinity"or holy living, therefore, recognizes the intregal relationship between beliefs and behavior,
faith and works. It is not a diminishing of the importance of
beliefs.

A Conflict of Gods

A character in James Michener's *The Source* suffers the
consequences of her husband's devotion to the wrong god. She
grieves the loss of her son who was sacrificed to the god Melak.
Now her husband celebrates the harvest by visiting the temple
prostitute. Michener describes the woman's mood as she is obvi-
ously deeply pained by her husband's behavior in the name of

religion. "And while others celebrated she walked slowly homeward, seeing life in a new and painful clarity: with different gods her husband . . . would have been a different man."[6] We are shaped by our god(s). Whatever is ultimate to us is our god. As Martin Luther wrote, "Now, I say whatever your heart clings to and confides in, that is really your God."[7] Whatever we count on to give our lives meaning, purpose, value, and destiny is our god. Everyone, therefore, believes in something. We simply cannot survive without some value, person, story, ideas, or assumptions which give life coherent meaning and purpose.

The great conflicts are between competing gods, not between atheism and religion. Belief in God is no virtue. Everybody believes in some god, some ultimate value(s). As far as we know, Jesus never met an atheist. It was belief in god(s) that resulted in people calling for Jesus to be crucified; and it was Jesus's belief in God which led him to pray from the cross, "Father, forgive them; for they know not what they do" (Luke 23:34a, RSV). The religion of Saul of Tarsus led him to persecute followers of Jesus Christ, and Paul's faith in a different God led him to pen the words, "And now faith, hope, and love abide, these three; and the greatest of these is love" (1 Corinthians 13:13). The difference was in the *nature* of the God who shaped Paul's life.

The *nature* of the God or gods we believe in and cling to is the critical issue. Belief in god(s) accounts for some of history's most diabolical crimes, and belief in God explains history's most noble deeds. Adolf Hitler wrote in *Mein Kampf*: "Hence today I believe that I am acting in accordance with the will of the Almighty Creator: *by defending myself against the Jews, I am fighting for the work of the Lord.*"[8] The attempt to exterminate the Jews, a people defined by their faith in the God of the Exodus, was driven by a belief system which claimed loyalty to God. However, it was Dietrich Bonhoeffer's belief in God that caused him to give his life in an attempt to counter Hitler and Nazism. It was the belief that God had consigned some human beings to inferiority and servitude that supported the buying and selling of human beings as slaves; and it was the conviction that all persons are equal before God and loved infinitely by God that led others, including John Wesley, to consider slavery a sin against God and humanity.

A disparity often exists between the beliefs we consciously affirm and those on which we act. The gods which shape our lives and the God affirmed in our creeds are not always the same. Holding an intellectual belief in God falls short of having faith in God. Jesus distinguished between those who say "Lord, Lord" and those who do "the will of my Father" (Matthew 7:21, RSV). John Wesley once said that he had met only two atheists in the British Isles; however, he observed that many "Christians" live "without God in the world." Those who profess belief in God but act without reference to God Wesley called "practical atheists."[9]

Jean-Paul Sartre, a philosopher who has influenced modern thinking about religion, writes: "Existentialism isn't so atheistic that it wears itself out showing that God doesn't exist. Rather, it declares that even if God did exist, that would change nothing."[10] Many people believe in God in the same way they believe in the existence of life on other planets: There may be such a thing, but it makes no difference in how they live. They are practical atheists. Or, more accurately, they affirm the possible existence of God but other gods shape their lives.

Multiple gods compete for our loyalty. *Polytheism* (belief in many gods) and idolatry are as prevalent among modern church members as they were among the ancient Canaanites. We feel torn by conflicting values. It is difficult to act with singleness of motive and commitment. Maintaining belief in the God who is concerned about, present with, and working for the healing of creation is not easy. Being shaped by the God present as Father, Son, and Holy Spirit demands considerable discernment and intentionality in today's world.

Popular Rivals to the God of Jesus Christ

Seldom is idolatry an explicit and intentional following of gods other than the one in which we affirm belief. If God is whatever "our hearts cling to" and whatever shapes our living, then we may identify our idols by asking: What really determines my decisions and actions? What is of supreme importance to me? What realities mold and shape my life? What does my heart cling to? For most of us, the answers are complex. Many ideas, relationships, values, stories, and goals influence us. We are not even conscious of all that shapes us. Seldom do we identify the reasons for our being, behaving, or believing. Much of the motivation is subconscious or unknown. Who we are and what we do result from multiple cultural, family, and personal realities.

Few people in our society consciously and explicitly reject the God revealed in the Exodus and in Jesus Christ. However, few people—if any—can claim to be shaped *totally* by such a God. Being shaped by the God of our creeds is very difficult and rare today. God has many appealing and subtle rivals. Here are a few of the gods that influence all of us.

Success

Success defined as achieving, accumulating, and receiving applause is a popular god. The temptation to center our lives in what we own, or know, or can do is pervasive. Our society tends to value persons in terms of their possessions, titles, looks, educational degrees, economic productivity, and professional or political power. Competition is valued above cooperation. Winning and advancing consume our energy and resources as individuals and institutions. Right and wrong are determined by what contributes to success. People become instruments or stepping stones to achievement. Personal well-being and national security are measured by ranking.

The Bible invites us to be shaped by a different God than success. Jesus warned that "many who are first will be last, and the last will be first" (Matthew 19:30). He challenged us to find life by losing it (Matthew 10:37-39) and to avoid seeking the "chief seats." According to Jesus, the meek shall inherit the earth. Greatness is in serving rather than being served. "Life does not consist in the abundance of possessions," he affirmed (Luke 12:15). His own temptation in the wilderness was a struggle with the success god as he defeated the tempter's challenge to root his life in prestige, popularity, and political power.

Consumerism

Consumerism is another seductive god. This god converts everything into a commodity to be marketed and consumed. Dr. Douglas Meeks contends that the market logic has become a pervasive idol of our time.[11] It values everything in terms of exchange. All relationships are utilitarian. They are evaluated on the basis of what one receives from them. The Biblical concept of 'dominion' is interpreted to mean the right of humans to exploit the earth. The ability to dominate has become a measure of one's power and importance. Consumerism reduces even God to a commodity to be used as a solution to personal problems or a means to selfish ends. God is portrayed as an instrument of one's happiness, success, and peace of mind rather than as One who invites us to join the reign of justice, righteousness, and joy.

Much in the contemporary church reflects the idolatry of consumerism. Many people join the church simply because of what it has to offer them. Churches become competitors vying for a greater share of the religious market. Evangelism is reduced to a marketing strategy for the recruitment of members rather than the proclamation of the good news of God's redemptive action in Jesus Christ. Worship is evaluated on the basis of its ability to attract the masses rather than being an offering the worshiper brings to God. Discipleship and mission become options in the church's schedule of multiple options, including recreational and entertainment activities. A church's faithfulness is judged by its size and how it meets the self-defined needs of its participants rather than being judged by how closely it fulfills its mission to be a visible sign and instrument of God's reign in Jesus Christ.

Consumerism runs counter to belief in God as the Creator and human beings as stewards. If this is "my Father's world" then we are responsible to God for our participation in creation. Since God desires that all creation live in harmony and all persons be treated with justice and compassion, there is a higher standard than my own needs or desires that masquerade as needs. As the sovereign of creation, God is to be worshipped and served. We are means to God's ends, not the reverse. The church exists to fulfill God's mission rather than to further our narcissistic goals. Jesus warned, "For what will it profit them to gain the whole world and forfeit their life?"(Mark 8:36). He defined authentic life in terms of the willingness to give it up and declared that discipleship includes the willingness to "sell all that you own and distribute the money to the poor" (Luke 18:18-25, also see Luke 14:33).

Wesley considered the accumulation of wealth and consumerism to be perhaps the most serious threats to the Christian gospel in general and the Methodist movement in particular. His famous sermon "On the Use of Money" is a call to avoid consumerism by adopting a simple lifestyle and giving to the poor. He believed that becoming a Christian makes one diligent and frugal, which in turn tends to result in growing wealthier. He contended that as people increase in riches they decrease in grace. They become distracted from the pursuit of holiness of heart and life, assume a stance of self-sufficiency, and separate themselves from the poor. In order to avoid the temptations of consumerism and wealth, early Methodists were urged to build plain meeting houses, limit their expenditures only to the necessities, and give the remainder to the poor. For Wesley, anything we have that is superfluous is a form of robbery of the poor. The early Methodists believed that sharing in the life of the self-giving God of Jesus meant sharing in the life of the poor and avoiding the seduction of consumerism.

Hedonism

Hedonism is another popular god which molds and shapes our lives. *Webster's New Collegiate Dictionary* defines hedonism as "the doctrine that pleasure or happiness is the sole or chief good in life."[12] The pursuit of pleasure, the avoidance of struggle, and the attainment of 'peace of mind' become the primary goals. Right and wrong depend upon feelings. "If it feels good, do it." Or, "it must be right if it feels right." Relationships, beliefs, activities are judged by their ability to bring pleasure and make one happy. God is reduced to a facilitator of good feelings, a means of avoiding suffering and struggle, and a champion of personal happiness. The church becomes a religious spa, the effectiveness of which is judged by its ability to solve personal problems and create positive feelings.

The Bible and our Wesleyan tradition emphasize happiness. In the Beatitudes of Jesus (Matthew 5:1-12) *blessed* can be translated *happy*. Jesus's definition of happiness, however, represents a contrast to hedonism. The Bible considers happiness as a serendipity, a by-product of a life shared with the God of Jesus Christ. Happiness results from commitment to Jesus Christ who said, " . . . whoever does not take up the cross and follow me is not worthy of me. Those who find their life will lose it, and those who lose their life for my sake will find it"(Matthew 10: 38-39).

John Wesley combined *happiness* with *holiness*. Wesley considered happiness a dimension of true religion. He proclaimed, "But true religion, or a heart right toward God and man, implies happiness as well as holiness."[13] But he claimed that there is no happiness apart from holiness; and holiness is the result of sharing in God's righteousness. He wrote, "This holiness and happiness, joined in one, are sometimes styled in the inspired writings, 'the kingdom of God' . . . because it is the immediate fruit of God's reigning in the soul."[14] *Happiness in the Wesleyan tradition, then, is the by-product of our relationship with God, the participation in God's reign of justice, compassion, and righteousness.* Only those who "strive first for the kingdom of God and his righteousness" (Matthew 6:33) have authentic happiness as a serendipity of commitment.

Popular Gods Distort Reality

Among other popular gods which are shaping our lives are *nationalism*, the worship of the nation; *individualism*, which extols the individual to the detriment of the community; *rationalism*, which exalts reason to the extreme by disallowing revelation and mystery; *racism* and *sexism*, which assign worth according to race and gender and use power to maintain one's own privileged position; *violence*, which considers that 'might makes right' and relies upon violence for security and self-esteem; and *institutional religion*, which confines God's presence and activity in religious institutions and gives religious rituals and doctrines priority over justice, mercy, and compassion.

The idols of success, consumerism, hedonism, nationalism, individualism, rationalism, racism and sexism, violence and institutional religion distort reality, destroy creation and community, and create enormous suffering. Such idols are causing the deaths of millions of people each year from poverty. Idolatry is killing millions by violence and depleting the earth's resources. Although adequate resources exists to provide for the basic needs for food, shelter, education, medical care, and clothing to all people on earth, the pursuit of false gods is resulting in millions of God's children being deprived of those necessities.

It matters which God or gods one believes in, and whatever shapes our lives is truly our god (God). The problem with idols is that they distort reality, rob life of its ultimate meaning, and finally destroy life itself. They cut us off from the true God, in whose reign we and all people are invited to participate. It is important, therefore, that we "not believe every spirit, but test the spirits to see whether they are from God" (1 John 4:1). As one United Methodist theologian reminds us, "To believe in God is at once to disbelieve what is not of God."[15]

Conclusion

Beliefs matter! We are shaped by them. Our relationships with one another and with the earth itself are grounded in our assumptions, our values, our dreams, and our perceptions. Whatever molds our lives is our God. The God we affirm in our creeds is not always the God that shapes our lives. The relationship between beliefs and behavior is complex and multifaceted. Integrity requires compatibility between our creeds and deeds.

John Wesley contended that true religion was not correct religious doctrine and practice. Rather, it is love of God and neighbor made possible by grace. He wrote, "The nature of religion is so far from consisting in these, in forms of worship, or rites and ceremonies, that it does not properly consist in any outward actions of what kind so ever."[16] He adds, "For neither does religion consist in *orthodoxy* or *right opinions*; . . . A man may be orthodox in every point; he may not only espouse right opinions, but zealously defend them against all opposers; he may think justly concerning the incarnation of our Lord, concerning the ever blessed Trinity, and every other doctrine contained in the oracles of God" and still not be authentically religious.[17] Wesley proceeded to define true religion as loving God with all the heart, and with all the mind, and with all the soul, and with all the strength, and loving one's neighbor as one's self.[18]

Authentic religion for the Methodists is sharing the life of God whose love is poured out in Jesus Christ and whose Holy Spirit shapes us into the likeness of Christ and empowers us 'to be holy as God is holy.' Religion, then, is a relationship with a certain God. The character in James Michener's book knew the importance of belief in God: The husband would be a different man if he had a different god. Who is the God revealed in Jesus Christ and witnessed to in the Bible, the historic creeds, and the experience of the church?

Opportunities for Reflection

The following questions may be used by groups wishing to discuss the material in Chapter Two or by individuals wanting to reflect on issues raised within the chapter.

1. Can one believe *anything* and still be United Methodist?

2. How do you understand John Wesley's statement, "As to all opinions which do not strike at the root of Christianity, we think and let think?" How comfortable are you with this statement?

3. This chapter discusses how we are shaped by values and ideas. What ideas or values influence and shape you? Do some values compete for your loyalty to God? What indications do you see of the idols of success, consumerism, hedonism, nationalism, etc.?

Chapter Three

The God Whose Life We Share

In the book, *Night,* Elie Wiesel shares his experiences as a young prisoner in Nazi concentration camps. The anguish, suffering, and death experienced by Wiesel challenge the reader's confidence in the existence of a loving God. The basic religious question is raised by a fellow prisoner during the hanging of three people, including a child. The prisoners in the camp were all forced to march past the gallows and watch the youngster die. He had a face like an angel. Since his body was small, it took him longer to die. As the prisoners watched this barbaric, senseless, dastardly spectacle of a youngster struggling between life and death, someone asked, "Where is God?" Expressing his despair about God's apparent absence, Wiesel thought: "Where is He? Here He is—He is hanging here on this gallows. . ."[1]

Where is God?

Amid a world where suffering and death are universally real, the questions are inevitable and necessary: Who is God? Where is God? What is God doing, if anything? Such questions express the longing within the human spirit for some transcendent presence and meaning. Television daily brings anguished scenes of traumatic suffering into our homes. Needless starvation, unnecessary poverty, senseless violence and incurable diseases challenge our belief in a God who is both powerful and compassionate. Where is God? Surely God is other than the one who simply views the human tragedy from a detached distance.

Doubt is sometimes the most honest and authentic affirmation of faith. Questioning is a gift of God by which we "test the spirits to see if they are of God." The poet Tennyson wrote:

> *There is more faith in honest doubt,*
> *Believe me, than in half the creeds.*[2]

Since much of the world's needless suffering has roots in religion, questions about the nature, presence, and purposes of God belong at the center of religious reflection and devotion. Through faith, expressed in doubt and confrontation with the scarred hands and side of the crucified and risen Christ, the Apostle Thomas was able to declare with new understanding, "My Lord and my God!" (John 20:28)

The United Methodist doctrinal/theological statement affirms: "With Christians of other communions we confess belief in the triune God—Father, Son, and Holy Spirit. This confession embraces the biblical witness to God's activity in creation, encompasses God's gracious self-involvement in the dramas of history, and anticipates the consummation of God's reign."[3] It is the Trinity—Father, Son, and Holy Spirit—that provides the grounding for knowing and relating to God. For Christians, the ambiguous word "God" comes into specific focus in the Triune name and in the cross, where the questions "Who is God?" and "Where is God?" are answered with shattering clarity. The Trinity is the narrative description of God who is a communion of love and freedom into which we are invited to participate. God is *before* us; God is *for* us; God is *with* us.

Faith is principally a relationship with God—a loving and reverent relationship of trustful obedience. Inquiry into God and relationship with God, however, do not take place in a vacuum or without resources. It is a primary affirmation that God has taken the initiative to disclose the divine character, action, and presence. God has responded to our longings, questions, and doubts. *Jesus Christ, as witnessed to in Scripture and in the church, understood through reason and experience, and in whose life and ministry we share through the Holy Spirit is God's answer to the question "Where is God now?"*

Jesus Christ, God for Us

Central to the Christian faith is the conviction that Jesus Christ is the supreme revelation of God. Our doctrinal statement affirms:

> At the heart of the gospel of salvation is God's incarnation in Jesus of Nazareth. Scripture witnesses to the redeeming love of God in Jesus' life and teachings, his atoning death, his resurrection, his sovereign presence in history, his triumph over the powers of evil and death, and his promised return. . . .
>
> Through faith in Jesus Christ we are forgiven, reconciled to God, and transformed as people of the new covenant.[4]

Jesus Christ is the very flesh and blood of God's nature and God's intention for all humanity. Jesus of Nazareth is the human face and action of the Father, Creator of the universe made known in history. John's Gospel proclaims: "And the Word became flesh and lived among us, and we have seen his glory, the glory as of a father's only son, full of grace and truth. . . . From his fullness we have all received, grace upon grace" (John 1:14, 16). Charles Wesley's beloved Christmas hymn expresses the Church's understanding of Jesus Christ:

> Christ, by highest heaven adored;
> Christ, the everlasting Lord,
> late in time behold him come,
> off-spring of a virgin's womb.
> Veiled in flesh the God-head see;
> hail th'incarnate Deity,
> pleased with us in flesh to dwell,
> Jesus, our Emmanuel.[5]

Persons who join The United Methodist Church are asked to accept Jesus Christ as *Lord* and *Savior*. He is both "the everlasting Lord" and "our Emmanuel." Accepting Jesus Christ as Lord means to live in terms of the sovereignty of Christ over all creation. As the revelation of God and God's purpose for humanity, Jesus Christ merits our full devotion, loyalty, and confidence. His life, teachings, death, resurrection, and ascension are the ultimate source of our understanding of ourselves, other people, the world, and the meaning and destiny of life. As the embodiment of the Everlasting God, the Creator of heaven and earth, Jesus Christ can be trusted, obeyed, and followed.

When asked what it means to accept Jesus Christ as Lord, a youth responded, "It means Jesus is the boss." Jesus Christ is more than "the boss," the one to be obeyed. The initial response of the first disciples was to the invitation, "Follow me." The invitation was not primarily to follow a set of rules nor to believe certain doctrines. It was the invitation to a relationship—a transforming friendship. The one who is *Lord*—Sovereign—is also *Savior.* He is the one who enables us to be and do that which he commands. In Jesus Christ, God entered the human struggle with sin and death which thwart the divine intention for life.

In the crucifixion Jesus confronted and absorbed the consequences and power of sin and death. The cross represents the results of sin and suffering and God's response to them. Christ on the cross gives new meaning to Elie Weisel's declaration of despair, "There God is, on the gallows." God is not absent! God has taken on the powers of evil and sin and *God has won!* The resurrection of Jesus Christ is God's eternal and resounding *no!* to the principalities and powers of darkness. The ascension of the risen Christ is God's promise to complete the victory begun in Jesus Christ. As we affirm in The Great Thanksgiving during Holy Communion, "Christ has died; Christ is risen; Christ will come again."[6]

Because Jesus Christ has entered the struggle with sin and death, and emerges triumphant, we can face our own sin and death with forgiveness and hope. Because God has won the ultimate victory, nothing in all creation is able to separate us from the love of God in Christ Jesus our Lord (Romans 8:39). In the power of the Holy Spirit, through baptism, we are incorporated into the death and resurrection of Jesus Christ and become part of the new humanity God is creating. We have been made brothers and sisters of Christ and one another. The God who is *for* us

in Jesus Christ has grafted us into the Divine life and mission
and is forever *with* us in the Holy Spirit.

The Holy Spirit, God With Us

United Methodists affirm in "A Modern Affirmation":

> *We believe in the Holy Spirit*
> *as the divine presence in our lives,*
> *whereby we are kept in remembrance*
> *of the truth of Christ,*
> *and find strength and help in time of need.*[7]

The Holy Spirit is God *with* us to comfort and convict, to
remind and renew, to guide and guard, to sustain and support.
Through the work of the Holy Spirit, we are convicted of our sin
and assured of forgiveness. We are reminded of Jesus Christ and
renewed in our relationship, guided toward the fulfillment of
God's purposes and guarded against the powers of sin and death.
In the power of the Holy Spirit we are sustained and supported
amid temptation, suffering, and death. It is the Holy Spirit who
draws us toward God and into community with God and one
another.

As one United Methodist scholar writes, "The Spirit is represented as the linking up of the life span of Jesus Christ, the
incarnate Word, with our own life span."[8] The test of whether a
spirit is the Holy Spirit is its conformity to Jesus Christ. (1 John
4:2ff) The fruits of the Spirit are the qualities of Jesus' own
being: "love, joy, peace, patience, kindness, generosity, faithfulness, gentleness, and self-control"(Galatians 5:22). Such qualities within and among human beings are God *with* us; they are
not human achievements or universal "natural" characteristics.
What we cannot produce in ourselves God produces in us–faith,
hope, and love or Christlikeness. Christopher Morse states it
well: "By the indwelling of the Holy Spirit, and not by any
alleged self-actualization of our own spirits, we relate to others
in ways that result in freedom and communion."[9]

The Holy Spirit is a gift which the God who is for us in
Jesus Christ bestows upon us. At Pentecost, the Spirit broke
down the barriers between human beings, loosened the tongues

of the apostles, and brought into being a new community. The Holy Spirit began shaping a community after the likeness of Jesus Christ and empowering it to be a sign, foretaste, and instrument of Christ's final victory. It is into that community, the church, that the Holy Spirit incorporates us. Through the guidance and strength of the Holy Spirit, the church becomes the "body of Christ" in mission to the world.

A hymn by Brian Foley prayerfully expresses the meaning and power of the Holy Spirit:

> *Holy Spirit, come, confirm us in the truth that*
> *Christ makes known;*
> *we have faith and understanding through your*
> *helping gifts alone.*
>
> *Holy Spirit, come, console us, come as advo-*
> *cate to plead;*
> *loving Spirit from the Father, grant in Christ*
> *the help we need.*
>
> *Holy Spirit, come, renew us, come yourself to*
> *make us live;*
> *holy through your loving presence, holy*
> *through the gifts you give.*
>
> *Holy Spirit, come, possess us, you the love of*
> *Three in One,*
> *Holy Spirit of the Father, Holy Spirit of the*
> *Son.*[10]

The Father, God Before Us

For more than sixteen hundred years, Christians have declared in the words of The Apostles' Creed: "I believe in God the Father Almighty, maker of heaven and earth . . ." The first of the Methodist Articles of Religion reads, "There is but one living and true God, everlasting, without body or parts, of infinite power, wisdom, and goodness; the maker and preserver of all things, both visible and invisible. And in unity of this Godhead there are three persons, of one substance, power, and eternity—the Father, the Son, and the Holy Spirit."[11]

The God who is *for* us in Jesus Christ and *with* us in the Holy Spirit is also *before* us as the Creator of heaven and earth. The mighty acts of salvation in Jesus Christ into which we are incorporated through the Holy Spirit have their origin in the One who brought creation into being. The One by whose power Mary conceived a Son is the One whose "wind swept over the face of the waters" and formed the earth out of the "formless void and darkness" (Genesis 1:2). The Power who brought forth Jesus Christ from the death and darkness of the tomb also called forth creation from chaos and nothingness. The One who created the heavens and the earth, redeemed and reconciled all things in Jesus Christ, and is present with us is bringing a new heaven and a new earth through the power of the Holy Spirit.

Since all creation has its origin and destiny in God, everything is dependent and contingent upon God. The highest value of any part of creation lies in the purpose assigned to it by the Creator. Human beings are stewards, cultivators, nurturers, and preservers of creation. God the Creator has invited us to share in the divine creativity and the ongoing efforts to bring healing and wholeness to creation, now scarred and wounded by human sin and continuing chaos.

The affirmation of God as Father is not a declaration of God's gender. It is a statement about God's power which brings all creation into being *and* the quality of God's relationship with creation, especially human beings. God is neither male nor female; God is "without body or parts." However, the Creator is not an impersonal or detached power, like electricity; God is personally and intimately involved with that which is created, like a mother and father with their children, or an artist with her painting, or a potter with his clay.

The Suffering God

Amid the grotesque cruelty and traumatic suffering of World War II, a German pastor/theologian, Dietrich Bonhoeffer, was hanged in a Nazi concentration camp. Before his death, Bonhoeffer wrote, "The Bible directs man to God's powerlessness and suffering; only the suffering God can help."[12] That is precisely the distinguishing and defining quality of the God of the Bible. God the Father, the Son, and the Holy Spirit is a suffering God who feels the pain and anguish of the world and its people. In the Exodus and in the cross, God is revealed as both Liberator and Suffering Servant who sees the misery of the people, hears their cries on account of their taskmasters, experiences their sufferings, and comes to deliver (Exodus 3:7-8). In the words of the philosopher Alfred North Whitehead: "God is the Great Companion–the fellow sufferer who understands."[13]

A unique characteristic of the God of the Bible is vulnerability to suffering, grief, and anguish. Whereas the gods of other cultures and religions were viewed as invincible and removed from the sufferings of the world, the God of the Hebrew Scriptures and the New Testament is portrayed as One who enters the sufferings of people. In fact, God is revealed as having an especially close relationship with those who suffer and are oppressed. God chooses the least—the most vulnerable, the powerless—as special messengers and means of accomplishing divine purposes. When a community was chosen to be a "light to the nations" (Isaiah 49:6), it was a band of powerless slaves. The chosen leaders were most often the youngest—the least prominent. The welfare and well-being of the chosen ones depended upon their executing justice and compassion for God's special friends—the poor, orphans, widows, sojourners, and strangers.

When God entered human flesh it was as a vulnerable baby, born of a young peasant mother. His first bed was a cattle stall. He was among the homeless. He spent the first months of his young life with his family as an alien in Egypt. He grew up in a working-class family and provided for the family by working with his hands in a carpenter's shop. When he began his public ministry, he called ordinary folks as disciples. The purpose of his ministry was announced as "to bring good news to the poor . . . to proclaim release to the captives and recovery of sight to the blind, to let the oppressed go free, to proclaim the year of the Lord's favor" (Luke 4:18-19). He so closely identified with the poor, the imprisoned, the sick that "just as you did it to one of the least of these . . . you did it to me" (Matthew 25:40).

This Messiah of God associated with outcasts, the sick, the poor, the disreputable, women, and children. He healed the sick, fed the hungry, raised the dead, wept with a grieving family, touched the untouchable lepers, pronounced forgiveness to the sinful, restored sight to the blind, blessed children, challenged the self-righteous, prayed for his executioners, and died among thieves. This is God *for* us, God *with* us, and God *before* us!

Where is God now? "There God is on the gallows!" God suffers *both* as the Son crucified and as the Father who enters the pain of a crucified and beloved child.

What is God doing? God is sharing the suffering, grief, anguish, and death of the world—and working to overcome it. God as the Holy Spirit is working to bring healing, reconciliation, and wholeness to all creation. Therefore, we can face our own and the world's suffering, sin, and death with confidence, knowing that the crucified and risen God is *for* us, *with* us, and goes *before* us.

Conclusion

The writer of Ephesians issues the gospel's most important challenge: "Therefore be imitators of God, as beloved children, and live in love, as Christ loved us and gave himself up for us, a fragrant offering and sacrifice to God" (Ephesians 5:1).

As we affirmed in Chapter Two, *the greatest threat to Christian discipleship is not atheism; it is idolatry, being shaped by and imitating the wrong god(s).* Many gods compete for our loyalty and devotion. They capture our attention and shape our lives sometimes without our awareness and conscious permission. Gradually we take on the nature of the god in whom we trust. Therefore, *the kind of god we trust is crucial.*

We have been created to share communion with God, a particular God: God the Father, the Son, and the Holy Spirit. The God whose life we share is *before* us as the Creator on whom all life depends and toward whose new creation all life will be judged. In Jesus Christ, God became incarnate and triumphed through and over suffering, sin, and death. This same God is present with us as the Holy Spirit to comfort, convict, guide, support, and sustain.

The last words of John Wesley prior to his death on March 2, 1791 at the age of eighty-eight were, "The best of all, God is

with us."[14] The day before, the weak and feeble leader of the
Methodist movement startled those attending him when he began
singing Isaac Watts' hymn, "I'll praise my Maker while I've
breath." The hymn describes the appropriate response to the God
who had shaped Wesley's life and ministry among "the people
called Methodist."

> *I'll praise my Maker while I've breath,*
> *and when my voice is lost in death,*
> *praise shall employ my nobler powers.*
>
> *My days of praise shall ne'er be past,*
> *while life, and thought, and being last,*
> *or immortality endures.*
>
> *Happy are they whose hopes rely*
> *on Israel's God, who made the sky*
> *and earth and seas, with all their train;*
>
> *whose truth forever stands secure,*
> *who saves th'oppressed and feeds the poor,*
> *for none shall find God's promise vain.*
>
> *The Lord pours eyesight on the blind;*
> *the Lord supports the fainting mind*
> *and sends the laboring conscience peace.*
>
> *God helps the stranger in distress,*
> *the widow and the fatherless,*
> *and grants the prisoner sweet release.*
>
> *I'll praise my God who lends me breath;*
> *and when my voice is lost in death*
> *praise shall employ my nobler powers.*
>
> *My days of praise shall ne'er be past,*
> *while life, and thought, and being last,*
> *or immortality endures.*[15]

Opportunities for Reflection

The following questions may be used by groups wishing to discuss the material in Chapter Three or by individuals wanting to reflect on issues raised within the chapter.

1. What does it mean to accept Jesus Christ as Lord and Savior?

2. Do you agree with Bonhoeffer's statement, "The Bible directs man to God's powerlessness and suffering; only the suffering God can help." Why? Why not?

3. What do you see as the greatest threat to Christian discipleship?

4. What are the implications of God's special friendship/relationship with the poor, the suffering, the vulnerable, and the outcast?

Chapter Four

Made in God's Image

Our beliefs about the nature, purposes, and activity of God shape and mold our lives. The kind of God we believe in and trust makes all the difference in the world. All existence is redefined by trust in the triune God, who is *for* us in Jesus Christ, *before* us as Father/Creator, and *with* us in the Holy Spirit. Commitment to the God who enters into suffering humanity and triumphs over sin and death transforms our understanding of ourselves and the world. Faithfulness requires that we persistently raise the critical questions: Who is God? Where is God? What is God doing?

Questions of equal importance are: Who are human beings? What is the purpose of human beings? What is their relationship to God and the creation of which they are part?

The ancient psalmist raised the issue this way:

> *When I look at your heavens, the work of your fingers,*
> *the moon and stars that you have established;*
> *what are human beings that you are mindful of them,*
> *mortals that you care for them? (Psalm 8:3-4)*

What we believe about human beings matters! Psychologists validate the importance of self-image in the formation of our identity and behavior. The role of anthropology (our understanding of human beings) in shaping society has been documented by sociology. How we treat ourselves and others—and how we form communities and nations—is determined by the image we have of human beings. It matters what we believe about the worth, value, purpose, and destiny of these creatures whom the psalmist declared God made "a little lower than God, and crowned them with glory and honor" (Psalm 8:5).

The Christian faith, as understood and practiced by the United Methodists, contradicts the assumption that human beings have their primary identity in their biology. Through the eternal Word in the power of the Holy Spirit, God has given us an identity that transcends biology, economics, or politics. As creatures made in the divine image by grace, human beings have been gifted with infinite worth, dignity, and destiny. Our identity lies in the One to whom we belong and in whose image we are made, not in how we look, what we know, or what we can do. God has created, redeemed, and claimed us as adopted children who participate in the divine presence and activity in the world. Therein lies our identity, worth, mission, and destiny!

A distinctive emphasis of Methodism from its inception is this: Human beings are made in the image of God and thereby share in God's own life and mission as a gracious gift of God. John Wesley's first 'university sermon,' preached in St. Mary's, the university church at Oxford, on November 15, 1730, was based on Genesis 1:27, RSV, "So God created man in his own image." This basic biblical affirmation formed the foundation of Wesley's doctrine of the 'way of salvation' as the primary agenda of Christian living. The Methodist's understanding of human beings, as made in the divine image, helped to account for their success among the poor and marginalized who had been stripped of their dignity and worth by alternative understandings. It is a message desperately needed in the impersonal and impoverished world of the twenty-first century.

The affirmation that God's grace is universal and that human beings have their basic origin in God makes political, geographic, ideological, and even religious distinctions subordinate to our common identity as creatures made in the divine image. John Wesley cautioned Methodists against bigotry, which he defined as, ". . . too strong an attachment to, or fondness for, our own party, opinion, Church, and religion."[1] Bigotry originates in the elevation of any group—political, ethnic, religious—above God's universal grace which creates humanity in the divine image.

Alternative Understandings of Human Beings

That the Creator of the heavens and the earth would bestow upon humans the status of being "a little less than God" was a source of astonishment and inspiration to the ancient psalmist. In the world of eighteenth-century England, the message that human beings were created in the image of the divine helped to spark a moral and religious revival. In a world now dominated by science, economics, and politics, such a lofty status ascribed to humans is exaggerated by some and denied by others.

It is not self-evident that humans are created in the divine image and share in the life of God. Sufficient evidence is available to support the notion that human beings are created in the likeness of the demonic. While standing in front of the gallows in a Nazi prison camp watching a child die, Elie Wiesel could have asked in addition to "Where is God?"[2] the corollary question, "Where is humanity?" Senseless violence, needless poverty, and calloused cruelty point to the absence of the divine image in the creatures the psalmist identifies as a little less than God.

Scientific developments and emerging economic and political trends raise new questions about the status and role of humanity. Humanity's distinctiveness in sharing God's life has been eroding for at least three hundred years. The astronomy of Galileo, Copernicus, and Newton challenged the notion of the earth's being the center of the solar system. The prevailing idea of an enclosed creation with the earth as central was replaced with a universe of infinite space and unfathomable distances. The earth has been reduced to a small planet among countless planets in a constellation of numberless galaxies. The poet's wonder is compounded: "When I look at your heavens . . . the moon and stars . . . What are human beings . . . ?" (Psalm 8:3-4).

Modern biology validates the kinship of human beings with other species. More than 98% of the molecules that make up the human being are shared by other species. As one scientist said to me, "We human beings have no reason to boast; we are only recycled atoms. The atoms in us have been in beasts, plants, birds, animals, and reptiles." Adequate reason exists to question the traditional "species chauvinism" which has motivated much human exploitation of creation. Human similarity with the rest of life is irrefutable. Indeed, the psalmist reminds us that we are "dust." Our days are like "grass" and "a flower of the field" (Psalm 103:14-16).

The identification and manipulation of the approximately 100,000 genes in the human cell pose new questions about the extent of human freedom and the source of human worth and identity. The ability of scientists to create, alter, or end life challenges the traditional religious understanding of life as a gift of a sovereign God. *What does it mean to be made in the image of God when humans can create, change, or end human life?*

Human beings are biological creatures. Many characteristics that distinguish us from one another are biological—skin color, gender, height, weight, facial features, physical stamina and health, brain capacity, and many personality traits. Behavior, attitudes, and perceptions have biological roots. Unknown and unchosen genetic influences help to shape our identity. Human beings are complex, interrelated biological organisms—a collection of appetites, drives, and atoms.

Defining Human Essence

Are human beings to be defined, valued, or treated primarily in terms of their biological qualities? Do genes and atoms decide our destiny? Are we to be judged by our race or gender, our mental capacity, physical shape or stamina? Are persons to be ranked by how they look, or what they know, or what they can do? Is our own sense of worth and our treatment of other people dependent upon biological characteristics? Is the meaning of life to be found in satisfying biological needs and appetites? Is there any existence beyond biological death and decay?

In addition to their biological qualities, human beings have always been tempted to define themselves by *political affiliations* and to root their identity in nations, ethnicity, social classes, religious affiliations, and/or ideologies. Defining one's essence by national origin has been a favorite idolatry since human beings first formed themselves into political entities. Being American, German, French, Italian, Korean, Zimbabwean, Peruvian, Egyptian, or Israeli can easily become more important than being a child of God. When the nation's ethnicity or ideology become primary in determining our self-concept or our treatment of others, the primary source of human identity is denied. Our common kinship with God and other people is sacrificed to other gods. Distinctions between people become sources of conflict, competition, and coercion rather than gifts to be woven into the fabric of our common humanity and celebrated as signs of God's grace.

The Book of Jonah is an early judgment upon the assumption of superiority and the separation of peoples into "friends" and "enemies." Jonah assumed the superiority of his nation over his despised enemies, the people of Nineveh. He wanted their destruction. He was repulsed by the notion that God would have mercy on the Ninevites. Jonah learned, however, that *his enemies* were not *God's enemies.* God's mercy and compassion included those from whom Jonah sought to distance himself.

The Market Logic of Exchange

Another threat to our identity as persons made in the divine image is economics and the market logic of exchange.[3] Identity based upon economics values persons by what they have to exchange in the marketplace. Although exchange is an important, necessary component of our economic life, the logic of exchange has slipped into the human psyche as a means of defining the nature or purpose of human beings. The logic of exchange reduces persons to commodities and relationships to utilitarian transactions.

An illustration of the devastating consequences of evaluating human beings on the basis of exchange value is the comment of an eighty-year-old man. He is in declining health and unable to work. The aging process is diminishing his energy and he now relies on his family to do many things he once did. Confronting his growing physical limitations and increased dependency, he said with regret and almost despair, "I'm not worth anything. I'm no good to anyone now."

A society that defines persons in terms of what they have of value to exchange eventually leaves its members demoralized, depleted, and "useless." Highly prized, marketable traits or qualities—such as youthful appearance, physical stamina, mental acumen, and productivity—eventually wane for everyone. As they diminish, so do self-esteem, hope, joy, and meaningful relationships. Since such values are subject to forces beyond our control, persons who root their worth in them are always insecure.

The image of God in human beings is rooted in grace— God's unmerited, undeserved love. Our status as children of God is nothing we have or could earn. It is a gift bestowed, not an achievement reached. In the words of the psalmist:

> *Yet you [God] have made them a little*
> *lower than God,*
> *and crowned them with glory and honor.*
> *(Psalm 8:5)*

Self-identity and relationships, therefore, operate by the logic of grace rather than the logic of exchange and merit. Since being made in the divine image is a status God bestows and makes possible through the power of the Holy Spirit, our identity and worth are not contingent upon precarious things such as appearance, mental and physical stamina, productivity, or economic security.

But what does it mean to be made in the image of God?

Made in God's Image

The 'image of God' has been interpreted in differing ways in the history of the church. Some interpretations have been destructive to humanity. They have resulted in the distortion of the divine image. For example, it has been contended that the 'divine image' has to do primarily with dominion over the rest of creation. The consequence has been the exploitation of creation by human beings. Or, some have used 'made in God's image' as a statement about gender, implying male superiority and dominance. Both distortions pervert the meaning of the doctrine and provide a theological rationale for actions and relationships that are contrary to the nature of God.

John Wesley saw *imago Dei*—image of God—in three manifestations:

1. The *natural image*, in which the human capacity for understanding, freedom of the will, and love are expressions of God's image;
2. The *political image*, in which human beings exercise stewardship over creation and share in God's ongoing governance of the earth; and
3. The *moral image*, in which the human potential for righteousness, true holiness, and happiness are signs of the divine image.[4]

For Wesley, the image of God denotes the human capacity for knowing and responding to God's grace. He proclaimed: "It was free grace that 'formed man of the dust of the ground, and breathed into him a living soul,' and stamped on that soul the image of God."[5]

Being created in God's image has to do primarily with relationship rather than with inherent qualities within human beings. God has created and called human beings to live in covenant fidelity with God the Father, the Son, and the Holy Spirit. As the triune God is defined by Oneness in the diversity of the relationship between the Father, Jesus Christ, and the Holy Spirit, *human beings are relational creatures whose basic identity is known only in relationship with the triune God.* Our origin is in God who claims and calls us. Our destiny is in being conformed to the image of Jesus Christ by the power of the Holy Spirit.

Origin, Calling, Identity and Destiny

The image of God is a declaration of the depth of our relationship with and dependences upon God. By the power of the Holy Spirit we are incorporated into the life and destiny of Jesus Christ, who is " . . . the image of the invisible God" (Colossians 1:15). Human beings are creatures created and claimed by God, called to conform to the likeness of Jesus Christ (2 Corinthians 3:18), and whose bodies are "a temple of the Holy Spirit" (1 Corinthians 6:19). Being made in the image of God means: We are created by God with the capacity to know and love God and one another; we have been incorporated into the life and destiny of Jesus Christ; and the Holy Spirit dwells within us as One who is ever working to conform us to the likeness of Christ, who is the true image of God. The vocation of every human being is to be "in such relationship to the origin, the provision, and the end of all creation that God appears through us."[6] Or, as we sing in the beloved hymn "Have Thine Own Way, Lord":

> *Have thine own way Lord!*
> *Have thine own way!*
> *Hold o'er my being absolute sway.*
> *Fill with thy Spirit till all shall see*
> *Christ only, always, living in me![7]*

The writer of the First Epistle of John summarized the identity, calling, and destiny of human beings in these words:

> *See what love the Father has given us, that we*
> *should be called children of God; and that is*
> *what we are. The reason the world does not*
> *know us is that it did not know him. Beloved, we*
> *are God's children now; what we will be has not*
> *yet been revealed. What we do know is this:*
> *when he is revealed, we will be like him, for we*
> *will see him as he is (3:1-2).*

As creatures in the divine image, our origin, calling, identity, and destiny are in Christ who is the image of God.

Conclusion

In many ways, human identity is formed by relationships. We take on the values, qualities, dreams, and goals of those to whom we relate in significant and ongoing ways. Critical to the health and wholeness of persons is a loving relationship with parents, those who gave us life. Parents give us our genetic traits that form much of our identity and destiny. They birth us into a family with a story and a constellation of relationships. We are shaped by relationships other than with parents—brothers and sisters, friends and colleagues, spouses and children. Out of these relationships emerge our own identity and destiny.

There is a relationship that goes before, permeates, and transcends our relationships with family, friends, and colleagues. It is the primal relationship that shapes and molds all others. It is our relationship with the triune God. Our origin is in God who created humanity in the divine image; called human beings to a common vocation of being the reflection of God's likeness; incorporated human beings into the life and destiny of Jesus Christ; and empowers us by the power of the Holy Spirit to conform to the One who is "the image of the invisible God, the firstborn of all creation."(Colossians 1:15)

Our identity as made in God's image is denied by much in the contemporary world and in our own experience. Other sources of defining who we are seem more compelling and self-evident. We are bombarded with messages that we are our biological needs, drives, and characteristics; therefore, fulfillment comes from satisfying our biological impulses and preserving and/or enhancing our biological assets. The temptation to root our identity and destiny in our national and ethnic origins or our ideological or religious affiliations is pervasive and persuasive. Being an American or a United Methodist becomes more important than celebrating and living our identity as children of God. The exchange logic of consumerism promises self-fulfillment in having, accumulating, consuming. Everything, including relationships and even God, becomes a commodity to be used to fulfill our self-defined goals.

Although made in God's image, human beings have accepted other identities and destinies. The result is the distortion of true humanity and the refusal of God's invitation to share in God's own life and mission in the world. Made with the capacity for living in covenant fidelity with God, humanity has turned toward relationships with gods other than the Creator. The divine image is distorted. Made "a little lower than God, and crowned . . . with glory and honor" (Psalm 8:5) human beings have settled for far less than their God-given identity and Christ-won destiny.

Opportunities for Reflection

The following questions may be used by groups wishing to discuss the material in Chapter Four or by individuals wanting to reflect on issues raised within the chapter.

1. Ponder a question raised in the text: What does it mean to be made in the image of God when humans can create, change, or end human life?

2. How do you define yourself? What affiliations, ideologies, and so forth are important in defining who you are?

3. What is your relationship to God? What difference does it make that our identity and worth are *gifts* from God, not *achievements*?

Chapter Five

The Divine Image Distorted

Humans are created for the purpose of sharing communion with the Triune God. Every person's primary vocation or calling is the fulfilling of his/her identity as an "adopted" child of God. Having been created and redeemed as children of God, we are to live in such relationship with our Creator, Redeemer, and Sustainer that God is made known in the world. The God who gives us such a lofty identity and destiny also shows us in Jesus Christ the perfect image of the divine. God does even more! Through the presence and power of the Holy Spirit, we are made part of the life and destiny of Jesus Christ and conformed into his likeness.

Something, however, has gone tragically wrong! Created to live in covenant fidelity with the triune God, human beings have betrayed the covenant, broken the relationship, and followed other gods. Made to live in freedom, we are enslaved by addictions and habits that distort the image of the God of liberation. Endued with the capacity to love as Jesus loves, we are caught in a web of selfishness, violence and exploitation that threatens human existence. Called to share in God's care and nurture of creation, humans plunder and poison the earth's resources, threatening its survival. Invited to share in the divine creativity by using gifts bestowed upon us by the Holy Spirit, we delight in defacing and degrading life's beauty and goodness. Promised "You shall be holy, for I the Lord your God am holy" (Leviticus 19:2), humanity defames and distorts God's nature, eschewing holiness of heart and life.

Our own experiences and observations provide ample evidence that more than God's image is at work in humanity. Gods other than the One known as Father, Son, and Holy Spirit shape and mold our lives. The Apostle Paul described the human condition in these words:

> For you did not receive a spirit of slavery to
> fall back into fear, but you have received a spirit
> of adoption . . . For the creation waits with
> eager longing for the revealing of the children
> of God . . . that the creation itself will be set free
> from its bondage to decay and will obtain the
> freedom of the glory of the children of God. We
> know that the whole creation has been groaning
> in labor pains until now; and not only the cre-
> ation, but we ourselves, who have the first fruits
> of the Spirit, groan inwardly while we wait for
> adoption, the redemption of our bodies.
> (Romans 8:15, 19, 21-22).

Our United Methodist doctrinal standards declare that sin is "the corruption of the nature of every man [human], that naturally is engendered of the offspring of Adam, whereby man [humanity] is very far gone from original righteousness, and of his own nature inclined to evil, and that continually."[1] The standards for doctrine also state, "We believe man [humanity] is fallen from righteousness and, apart from the grace of our Lord Jesus Christ, is destitute of holiness and inclined to evil."[2]

Sin is Real

The divine image in humanity is distorted by sin. John Wesley believed that every manifestation of God's image in human beings has been stained and perverted. The "natural image" with its capacity for understanding, freedom, and love has been permeated by confusion, bondage, and hatred. We are blind to the purposes and presence of God, captive to our own appetites and desires, and filled with selfishness, apathy and animosity. The "political image," which gives us the ability to share in God's care and nurture of the world, is distorted by greed and exploitation. Our potential for righteousness and holiness—the "moral image"—is twisted and defamed by pervasive evil that invades our thoughts, relationships, and actions.

In his sermon entitled, "The One Thing Needful," Wesley describes the condition of humanity:

> But sin hath now effaced the image of God. He [humanity] is no longer nearly allied to angels. He is sunk lower than the very beasts of the field. His soul is not only earthly and sensual, but devilish. Thus is the mighty fallen! The glory is departed from him! His brightness is swallowed up in utter darkness!
>
> From the glorious liberty wherein he was made he is fallen into the basest bondage. The devil, whose slave he now is, to work his will, hath him so fast in prison that he cannot get forth. He hath bound him with a thousand chains, the heavy chains of his own vile affections. For every inordinate appetite, every unholy passion, as it is the express image of the god of this world, so it is the most galling yoke, the most grievous chain, that can bind a free-born spirit. And with these is every child of Adam, everyone that is born into this world, so loaded that he cannot lift up an eye, a thought to heaven; that his whole soul cleaveth unto the dust![3]

Every part of humanity has been infected with sin. "Our body, soul, and spirit, are infected, overspread, consumed, with the most fatal leprosy. We are all over, within and without, in the eye of God, full of diseases, and wounds, and putrifying sores."[4]

Various explanations of the nature and origin of sin have been offered by theologians. Reinhold Niebuhr's account of sin as *pride* is well known. Sin is succumbing to the inevitable temptation to compete with God for dominance and control. It is thinking that we are gods rather than daughters and sons of God. But sin is also *sloth*, which makes us less than children of God.

It is the failure to *be* the image of God in which we have been created. Sin is falling short of our true identity and our refusal of kinship with the One in whose likeness we are made.

Sin is more than behavior or personal habits that can be changed with effort or simple remedy. Sin has to do with "missing the mark," failing to *be* who God invites us to be. It is reflecting other than the "image of God." It is a disease of the soul for which human beings cannot cure themselves. It disfigures, distorts, and thwarts God's intention for humanity.

Wesley rooted sin in the liberty that God bestowed upon human beings. He defined sin as a willful, voluntary transgression of the known will of God. Human beings have chosen to use their freedom in ways that deny kinship. Rather than accepting the invitation to share in God's life and mission, we declare independence from God and live in competition with and rebellion against the Creator.

Sin's Pervasive Power

The doctrine of *original sin* affirms that sin is inescapable, pervasive, and systemic. The Articles of Religion of The Methodist Church states: "Original sin standeth not in the following of Adam (as the Pelagians do vainly talk), but it is the corruption of the nature of every man [human being] . . ."[5] 'Original sin' further describes evil's power over humanity: "The condition of man [humanity] after the fall of Adam is such that he cannot turn and prepare himself, by his own natural strength and works, to faith . . ."[6]

The doctrine of original sin means that *sin has deeper roots than individual, personal choices.* Sin is so pervasive in human personality and in society that we cannot avoid captivity to it. Before we are conscious of having a choice, we have already become victims of sin. For example, we inevitably assume the values of the prevailing culture. Persons born into a society that views African-Americans as inferior become prejudiced without initially choosing to do so. Or, a male who grows up in an environment that assigns a subordinant role to women is likely to be sexist without realizing it. This disease of the soul—*sin*—infects all human beings. It invades every aspect of life. No areas of human existence are left untouched by sin's presence. Even our best remains tainted and fails to fulfill the divine image.

The power of sin exceeds human strength. It is more than a personal inclination or temptation that can be defeated by willpower. As the Apostle Paul wrote, "For our struggle is not against enemies of blood and flesh, but against the rulers, against the authorities, against the cosmic powers of this present darkness, against the spiritual forces of evil in the heavenly places" (Ephesians 6:12). Demonic forces pervade institutions, individuals, cultures, and systems. They create injustice, oppression, and cruelty; and we fall victim to their prey without realizing it. The insidious powers of sin and death assault humanity with weapons of deceit, treachery, coercion, manipulation, and violence. The results are the persistent distortion of the divine image in humanity, the breaking of covenant with God, and a creation threatened with destruction.

Reluctance to Acknowledge Sin

An adult Sunday School class in a United Methodist Church requested a session with the pastor. The class of young adults objected to the use of prayers of confession in the Sunday morning worship service. The reasons for their objections were these:

- *We are not guilty of some of the sins identified.*
- *The prayers either imply or state that "we are unworthy of God's love."*
- *Confession is negative and worship should promote positive feelings.*
- *Calling people sinners damages their self-image.*

When asked how they would account for the apparent evil in themselves and the world, members of the class talked in terms of "emotional problems," "psychological needs," "sickness," and "maladjustment." Therapy, personal discipline, and support groups were seen as more appropriate remedies for human imperfections than repentance and confession of sin.

The church's understanding of sin seems archaic to modern ears, even to the "people called Methodist"! Other explanations seem more sophisticated and plausible. Referring to men and women as *sinners* and calling harmful and hurtful behavior *sin* is considered to be insensitive, judgmental, and harsh. Understanding human beings as sinners is thought by some to cause psychological damage by preventing a positive self-image.

True, people can be damaged by an emphasis on sin. The misuse of the doctrine contributes to further distortion of the image of God in humanity. It can be interpreted so as to justify self-hate, judgmentalism, cruelty, and emotional sickness. Many people bear the scars of a "hellfire and damnation" religion that describes people as worthless sinners awaiting the eternal damnation and punishment of a wrathful God. The doctrine of original sin has also been used to justify negative attitudes toward sexuality and women.

The misuse of the doctrine of sin, however, does not warrant its removal from our vocabulary and understanding. Wesley confronted considerable resistance to his own preaching about sin. The emerging "age of reason" of the eighteenth century went to considerable lengths to counter the church's traditional arguments about human "depravity." The following excerpt from Wesley's sermon, "Original Sin" sounds as if it could have been written today. He began the sermon by acknowledging that teachers and preachers throughout history have provided glowing descriptions "concerning the nature of man [humanity], as if it were all innocence and perfection." He added:

> *Accounts of this kind have particularly abounded in the present century; and perhaps in no part of the world more than in our own country. Here not a few persons of strong understanding, as well as extensive learning, have employed their utmost abilities to show what they termed "the fair side of human nature." And it must be acknowledged that if their accounts of him be just, man is still but "a little lower than the angels . . ."[7]*

Wesley admitted that positive accounts of human nature are widely read and believed. He laments, "So that it is now quite unfashionable to talk otherwise, to say anything to the disparagement of human nature; which is generally allowed, notwithstanding a few infirmities, to be very innocent and wise and virtuous."[8] To ignore the reality of human sinfulness, according to Wesley, is to deny the Bible and human experience and to perpetuate human captivity to sin.

Whatever Became of Sin?

The eminent psychiatrist, Karl Menninger, wrote a book in 1973 entitled, *Whatever Became of Sin?*. Dr. Menninger called for a recovery of the doctrine of sin. He warned against designating all negative behavior and destructive traits in human beings as sickness or maladjustment. According to the psychiatrist, assuming that psychotherapy and medicine can cure every human ailment ignores and leaves untreated humankind's most serious problem—sin.[9]

In the early 1990s the *New York Times* carried a reprint of a *Wall Street Journal* editorial. The provocative editorial was followed by this tag line: "When was the last time you had a good conversation about sin?" The editorial referred to a number of the moral dilemmas appearing daily in the media. There followed this comment:

> *Sin isn't something that many people, including most churches, have spent much time talking about or worrying about through the years of the (cultural and sexual) revolution. But we will say this for sin; it at least offered a frame of reference for personal behavior. When the frame was dismantled, guilt wasn't the only thing that fell away; we also lost the guidewire of personal responsibility . . . Everyone was left on his or her own. It now appears that many wrecked people could have used a road map.*[10]

Sin Has Consequences

Wesley was correct in saying that the sinfulness of humanity can be denied only by ignoring the Bible and experience.

Certainly Scripture affirms the pervasiveness, power, and destructiveness of sin. From Genesis to Revelation, the drama of evil's power and humanity's refusal to share obediently and lovingly in God's own life and mission unfolds. The Bible is the story of human flight from the One in whom humanity finds its home. From Adam and Eve's hiding in guilt and shame, to Cain's murder of his brother, to the crucifixion of Jesus Christ, the distortion of the image of God in humanity appears as a constant theme in the biblical story. The New Testament declares, "all have sinned and fall short of the glory of God" (Romans 3:23), and "If we say we have no sin, we deceive ourselves, and the truth is not in us" (1 John 1: 8).

The tragic consequences of such distortion are revealed graphically in the cross. The crucifixion is more than the execution of an innocent man; it is dramatization of sin's power and consequences and God's response. Sin results in needless suffering of others– especially the innocent—and God. As the New Testament warns, "the wages of sin is death" (Romans 6:23). The consequence of persistent denial and betrayal of the divine image is suffering—the suffering of God. God so closely identifies with the human family that God assumes the suffering and death inflicted upon it. The cross of Christ, then, represents sin's tragic consequences upon humanity and upon God.

Daily Awareness of Sin

We are daily confronted with the consequences of sin. Scenes of needless suffering enter our homes through television: children dying from hunger and neglect caused by economic injustice, young men and women killed and wounded in war and violence, elderly persons suffering from loneliness, people caged in prisons and jails, the earth itself being poisoned and depleted, men and women addicted to drugs and alcohol, the homeless wandering the world's streets and roadways.

The distortion of the divine image has consequences more personal than scenes on television screens. Our own inner lives and relationships with those around us bear the scars of a distorted identity. An incessant anxiety stalks us. Feelings of inadequacy and fear of being unable to "measure up" drive us to compulsive competition and conspicuous consumption. Dread of growing old and dying robs us of hope and joy. Betrayal and neglect of covenants with spouses and children leave us ashamed and guilty. Tensions, mistrust, alienation and anger plague our relationships. Loneliness and meaninglessness invade us and defeat the optimism and mission which once pulled us toward the future. We often feel lost in a dangerous wilderness, away from home. The words of Charlotte Elliott's hymn describe our condition:

> *Just as I am, though tossed about,*
> *with many a conflict, many a doubt,*
> *fightings and fears within, without . . .*
>
> *Just as I am, poor, wretched, blind;*
> *sight, riches, healing of the mind,*
> *yea, all I need in thee to find.*[11]

Conclusion

The divine image in which human beings are made has been distorted and disfigured, causing enormous suffering and anguish to both humans and God. The failure to live in the image of God and share God's life and mission is the essence and origin of sin. Sin is universal, pervasive, and inescapable. Its power permeates every aspect of life and thwarts God's intention for all creation. The cross of Jesus Christ represents the tragic consequences of sin. Sin seeks the death and destruction of the image and purpose of God, who enters into the suffering and death of humanity.

But sin is not the last word! It is not the most powerful and pervasive reality in the universe! *What humanity cannot do– restore the divine image– God does.* The One who created us in God's image and invited us into covenant relationship takes the initiative to restore the image. In Jesus Christ God enters the wilderness to set humanity free and to lead the prodigal sons and daughters home. *God, in Christ, takes on the 'principalities and powers' and triumphs over them!*

John Wesley considered the restoration of the divine image to be the heart of authentic religion. He proclaimed: "Ye know that the great end of religion is to renew our hearts in the image of God, to repair that total loss of righteousness and true holiness which we sustained by the sin of our first parent."[12]

Where is God? The "crucified" God is wherever there is suffering and sin!

What is God doing? Through the power of the Holy Spirit and the redemptive life, death, and resurrection of Jesus, God is working to restore the divine image in humanity, bringing creation itself into conformity with Jesus Christ—the image of the invisible God.

What is the appropriate response to this God? Accept the grace of God which goes before us, saves us, and transforms us.

Opportunities for Reflection

The following questions may be used by groups wishing to discuss the material in Chapter Five or by individuals wanting to reflect on issues raised within the chapter.

1. In what ways does sin disfigure, distort, or thwart God's intention for your life? For your congregation? For the world?

2. In what ways can people be damaged by an emphasis on sin?

3. In what ways are you confronted with the consequences of sin?

Chapter Six

Reconciled and Transformed by Grace

The United Methodist doctrinal/theological statement confesses: "The created order is designed for the well-being of all creatures and as the place of human dwelling in covenant with God. As sinful creatures, however, we have broken that covenant, become estranged from God, wounded ourselves and one another, and wreaked havoc throughout the natural order. We stand in need of redemption."[1]

The essence and purpose of "real religion," says John Wesley, is "a restoration of man by Him that bruises the serpents's head to all that the old serpent deprived him of; a restoration not only to the favour but the likeness to the image of God . . . Nothing short of this is the Christian religion."[2] Wesley's principal concern was "the order of salvation." Albert Outler, one of the foremost Wesleyan scholars, wrote, "The controlling theological inquiry throughout his life was into the meaning of becoming and being a Christian in all the aspects of Christian existence."[3] Methodism is rooted in the belief that God seeks to reconcile all persons, remaking them into the image of Jesus Christ. In spite of humanity's distortion of the divine image and the betrayal of covenant fidelity, God the Creator is *for* us in Jesus Christ and *with us* in the Holy Spirit, and is always *before* us, bringing into being a new creation. The Methodist movement considered the sharing in God's reconciling and transforming action to be its mission. Both in England and America, early Methodists believed that God had raised them up "to reform the nation, particularly the Church, and to spread Scriptural holiness over the land."[4] Nothing short of participating in God's initiative to reclaim humanity and reform the whole of creation has formed the foundation of Methodism's existence.

Central to Methodism is an emphasis upon grace. "Grace pervades our understanding of Christian faith and life," affirms *The Book of Discipline.*[5] Although we share with other Christians a belief in salvation by grace, Methodist traditions have combined the manifestations of grace in a manner to create distinctive emphases for living the full Christian life. A recovery of those emphases can be a means by which we are reconciled to God and renewed in the image of God.

Grace Defined

The Book of Discipline defines grace as "the undeserved, unmerited, and loving action of God in human existence through the ever-present Holy Spirit."[6] The United Methodist Church's Mission Statement includes this definition: "The triune God is grace who in Christ and through the Holy Spirit prepares, saves, and makes a new people."[7] Grace *is* God sharing the divine life in creating, redeeming, and transforming all life after the image of Christ.

Wesley defined grace as God's "bounty, or favour: his free, undeserved favour, . . . man having no claim to the least of his mercies. It was free grace that 'formed man of the dust of the ground, and breathed into him a living soul,' and stamped on that soul the image of God, and 'put all things under his feet.' . . . For there is nothing we are, or have, or do, which can deserve the least thing at God's hand."[8]

Grace is God doing on our behalf what we could never do for ourselves—create ourselves in the image of God, reconcile ourselves to God whose life we have denied and distorted, restore the divine image in humanity, and transform ourselves and creation into the likeness of Jesus Christ. Grace is Jesus Christ! It is God's response to Paul's cry of despair, "Wretched man that I am! Who will rescue me from this body of death? Thanks be to God through Jesus Christ our Lord" (Romans 7:24-25). Grace is God, "who is rich in mercy, out of the great love with which he loved us even when we were dead through our trespasses, made us alive together with Christ—by grace you have been saved . . ." (Ephesians 2:4-5).

God's grace is universal and available to all persons. The divine presence and power permeate all of life with potential for beauty, goodness, truth, and love. Grace is God's gifts bestowed, God's gifts received, God's gifts shared, and God's gifts transforming. Living in accordance with grace orients life around God's gift of salvation. We trust that God is *before* us, *for* us, and *with* us in the journey toward the fulfillment of our identity and destiny.

Although grace is one as the triune God is One, grace in the Methodist tradition is understood as manifested in three actions:

- *Prevenient Grace*
- *Justifying (saving) Grace*
- *Sanctifying Grace*

Every stage on the journey toward salvation is made possible by God's grace.

Prevenient Grace—The Grace Before Us

Although Methodists recognize the seriousness of sin and the tragic distortion of God's image in humanity, Wesley believed that God's grace is present—"preventing" the total destruction of the divine image. Grace is present in all persons to prevent the complete distortion of God's image and to prepare persons for reconciliation and restoration. Prevenient grace is defined as ". . . the divine love that surrounds all humanity and precedes any and all of our conscious impulses. This grace prompts our first wish to please God, our first glimmer of understanding concerning God's will, and our 'first slight transient conviction' of having sinned against God."[9]

Prevenient grace is present in all creation—the natural order, in the human conscience, in the relationships into which we are born. The love of family, the Christian community, the sacraments, pangs of guilt, longings for meaning and purpose and love, awareness of our alienation are all vehicles of prevenient grace. *Each decision or response to God is preceded by God's own prompting and action. That is the essence of prevenient grace.*

Prevenient grace enabled early Methodists to proclaim the gospel boldly and confidently to persons marginalized by the world, such as the impoverished and the imprisoned. The Methodist preachers trusted that God was already present in the mines and slums, in the prisons and on the gallows, awakening persons to their identity as children of God. A "desire to flee from the wrath to come"[10] was the only requirement for membership in the Methodist Societies. That is, Methodism was open to those in whom *prevenient grace* was prompting, convicting, and drawing them toward the restoration of their true identity. Prevenient grace is the "prodigal son" in Luke's Gospel confronting his lost identity:

> *But when he came to himself he said, "How many of my father's hired hands have bread enough and to spare, but here I am dying of hunger! I will get up and go to my father, and I will say to him, 'Father, I have sinned against heaven and before you; I am no longer worthy to be called your son . . .'" (Luke 15:17-19).*

Wesley described prevenient grace as the *porch* on a house. It is the place where we prepare to enter the house. It is possible to live one's life on the porch, the very edges of home, with only glimpses of and longings for fellowship with the family. But God does not leave us on the porch, on the edges of home. As we live on the porch, we not only long to be in the house, but we feel unworthy of entering. God's grace, however, enables us to enter our true home and claim our place in the family.

Justifying Grace—Grace for Us

The *door* into the house of God's salvation is *justification*, or justifying grace. "Justification," said Wesley, "is another word for pardon. It is the forgiveness of all our sins, and . . . our acceptance with God."[11] Justifying grace is the assurance of forgiveness that comes from repentance, from turning toward God's gracious gift of life in Jesus Christ. It is being made right with God, being reconciled through Christ to the Creator whose covenant we have betrayed and whose image we have distorted.

The Book of Discipline affirms: "In justification we are, through faith, forgiven our sin and restored to God's favor. This righting of relationships by God through Christ calls forth our faith and trust as we experience regeneration, by which we are made new creatures in Christ."[12]

As prevenient grace is something God does *before* us, justifying grace is that which God does *for* us in Jesus Christ. We are adopted into the life, death, and resurrection of Jesus Christ who intercedes for us. What we cannot do—atone for our sins—Christ does for us. Justifying grace is God in Christ affirming that we are still daughters and sons of God. Faith is turning away from an identity shaped by idols and turning toward our kinship with God. It is taking personally what God has done for all humankind in Jesus Christ.

Wesley's description of his experience at Aldersgate Street is an example of justifying grace. After years of attempting to be reconciled to God by strict obedience and failing as a missionary in America, Wesley joined a small group of Christians who gathered at Aldersgate Street for Bible study and prayer. He wrote of the experience:

> *About a quarter before nine, while he [the leader] was describing the change which God works in the heart through faith in Christ, I felt my heart strangely warmed. I felt I did trust in Christ, Christ alone for salvation, and an assurance was given me that he had taken away my sins, even mine, and saved me from the law of sin and death.*[13]

Wesley insisted that faith in Christ is the sole necessary and sufficient cause of justification. Faith is trusting Christ's death as "for me." It is acting upon what God has done in Jesus Christ as the basis of our status with God. *Faith, trust in Christ, is also a gift from God and not a human achievement.* Assurance of pardon and our status as restored children of God are not dependent upon feelings. For Wesley, the assurance of justification was the evidence in the changed lives of those to whom God's justifying grace was proclaimed.

The process of justification and new birth as restored children of God is often referred to as *conversion,* which is the appropriation of justifying grace. It is a change in how we view ourselves, others, and the world around us. Our doctrinal/theological statement recognizes that "Such a change may be sudden and dramatic, or gradual and cumulative. It marks a new beginning, yet it is part of an ongoing process."[14]

Another term used to describe justification is *new birth* or *being born again.* As physical birth is a complex process with interrelated experiences, the *new birth* includes multiple components. No two births are identical. Spiritual birth begins with conception (*God's secret*) and continues in gestation (*justification*). Then comes birth (*justification*), followed by growth (*sanctification*) and maturity (*Christian perfection*). Each experience is inseparable from the others. All are shrouded in mystery and transcendence.

Justification is more than the forgiveness of our sin and the restoring of our personal relationship with God. Through justifying grace, we are incorporated into Christ's community in which people are accepted and affirmed as children of God. We become members of a new family in which kinship transcends genetics, geography—even religion. It is a community built upon and shaped by the person of Jesus Christ and the power of the Holy Spirit, not merit or earthly status. By accepting and affirming our God-given identity and destiny as children of God, we affirm our solidarity with all whom God loves and for whom Christ dies.

Realization that our worth, identity, kinship, and destiny are rooted in the God who is *before* us and *for* us is the essence of justifying grace. To accept that status and enter the doorway of a new creation is the beginning of our salvation. It is an identity—a destiny that we can never earn, nor can it be taken from us. God, however, does more with sin than forgive it. God's grace goes beyond giving us status as sons and daughters of God.

Sanctifying Grace—Grace Perfecting Us

God's goal for humanity is the complete restoration of the divine image and the total conformity of all creation to the image of Jesus Christ. *Sanctification* (from *sanctus,* holy) denotes the process by which the believer is made holy following justification.

The Book of Discipline states: "We hold that the wonder of God's acceptance and pardon does not end God's saving work, which continues to nurture our growth in grace. Through the power of the Holy Spirit we are enabled to increase in the knowledge and love of God and in love for our neighbor."[15]

Wesley referred to sanctification as the *grand depositum* of Methodism. For Wesley, justification is what God does *for* us— the forgiveness of sins and incorporation into a new community; sanctification is what God does *in* us—holiness of life. Justification begins the process of being conformed to the image of Christ. Through the power of the Holy Spirit, God creates in the believer "holiness of heart and life." Grace is not content to give us a new status before God; it creates in us a new being characterized by holiness.

The doctrine of Christian perfection represents a distinctive emphasis of historic Methodism. Methodist preachers have been asked since the days of Wesley: Have you faith in Christ? Are you going on to perfection? Do you expect to be made perfect in love in this life? Are you earnestly striving after it? These historic questions assume an understanding of "Christian perfection" or holiness of heart and life. They are not so much affirmations of human potential as they are affirmations of the power of God's grace in Jesus Christ to make us new creatures.

Sanctifying grace draws us toward the gift of Christian perfection, which Wesley described as a heart "habitually filled with the love of God and neighbor" and "having the mind of Christ and walking as he walked."[16] Sanctification is the process of maturing in discipleship until the heart is habitually inclined to do what is right. Perfection—sanctification or holiness—is not to be equated with *perfectionism* or flawlessness. Neither is it an achievement; it is a gift emerging from friendship with and obedience to Christ. One may never attain the state of sinlessness. Wesley, however, was convinced that it is possible to so love God that one loses the desire to sin and consistently live in the light of God's love.

Love is the definition of perfection. Wesley said, "This is the sum of Christian perfection: it is all comprised in that one word, love."[17] The promise and command in the Sermon on the Mount, "Be perfect, therefore, as your heavenly Father is perfect" (Matthew 5:48) follows the description of discipleship as including love for enemies. The commandments are all summed up in "You shall love the Lord your God with all your heart, and with all your soul, and with all your mind" (Matthew 22:37); and "You shall love your neighbor as yourself" (Matthew 22:39). Wesley understood the "commands" of Christ as "covered commands." What Christ commands, Christ *covers* with the promise to enable us to fulfill. In other words, *Christ does not command us to do what Christ does not empower us to do.*

Glorifying Grace—Personal and Social Transformation

Sanctifying grace seeks the total transformation of creation. Wesley strongly affirmed that there is no true holiness apart from social holiness. Restoring the image of God in individuals falls short of God's reign over all creation. The theme of Jesus' preaching and the broader framework of the Methodist movement was the kingdom of God. God is bringing a new world of justice, righteousness, generosity, and joy. Nothing less than a new heaven and a new earth conformed to Jesus Christ is God's vision for creation. The victory that God won in Jesus Christ will be consummated; and wherever God's righteousness exists, the Kingdom is already present.

Methodists have understood that the kingdom of God, announced and inaugurated by Jesus Christ, has tangible social consequences in society. The Kingdom is both *inward* in the heart of the believer and *outward* in the life of the world. The Kingdom is both a present reality *and* a future hope. It is present wherever God's will is done, wherever the love of God is manifested. The Kingdom is yet to come in its fullness. But God's glorifying grace will bring to completion God's final reign of righteousness, which is God's power over evil and death. Charles Wesley's beloved hymn expresses *both* dimensions of grace:

Finish, then, thy new creation; pure and spot-
less let us be.
Let us see thy great salvation perfectly restored
in thee;
changed from glory into glory, till in heaven we
take our place,
till we cast our crowns before thee, lost in won-
der, love, and praise.[18]

Sanctifying grace incorporates us into God's reign over sin and death and calls us to participate in God's transforming of creation. One United Methodist scholar writes: "This is what sanctification is all about—becoming an agent of the age to come, joining in the struggle against the forces of sin and corruption, claiming the promise of the new age and living in the hope that the victory over sin is indeed possible."[19] It was this understanding of sanctification and the reign of God that propelled the Methodists into social action. Since their origin, Methodists have been involved in education, medical care, economic and political issues, and human rights concerns *because of God's sanctifying grace which seeks to bring into being a whole new creation.* Wesley's involvement in issues of poverty, slavery, prison reform, human rights, education and medical care did not result from a political agenda or as mere happenstance. His involvement grew out of his evangelical vision of God's grace which transforms *all* of life and his confidence in the ultimate triumph of God's realm. As we affirm in "A Statement of Faith of The Korean Methodist Church":

We believe in the reign of God
as the divine will realized in human society,
and in the family of God,
where we are all brothers and sisters.
We believe in the final triumph of righteousness
and in the life everlasting.[20]

Conclusion

The distinctive Wesleyan emphasis upon salvation by grace spawned a spiritual revival in eighteenth century England and frontier America. The message of God's universal grace present and available to *all persons* struck a responsive note among people who had been demoralized by their own sin and the sin of society. The poor and outcast especially found hope, renewal, and transformation in the message that God the Creator who is *for* and *with* them will enable them to share in Christ's final victory over sin and death. God's prevenient, justifying, and sanctifying grace gave the Methodists their mission: to reform the nation, particularly the church, and to spread scriptural holiness throughout the land. By God's grace made flesh in Jesus Christ, they shared in the life and mission of God!

The emphasis upon prevenient, justifying, and sanctifying grace is desperately needed today. A generation that defines people by wealth, social status, academic degrees, professional achievements, physical appearance, and political power seeks wholeness (salvation) through having, doing, knowing, succeeding. The result is a secular form of "works righteousness" and its resulting despair and anxiety.

We need the affirmation that God has acted decisively in Jesus Christ to set us free from all idols and through the Holy Spirit continuously works to restore our identity as children of God. No longer do we have to *earn* our place in the world or *prove* our right to be. God has given us a place in God's own family and a part in God's mission to the world. In Jesus Christ the divine image has been restored. We now share in the restored image. We are surrounded by grace—God's unmerited favor—which prods, prompts, forgives, and perfects us in love.

Prevenient, justifying, and sanctifying grace are not sequential or chronological experiences. Neither are they one-time manifestations of grace. Every moment is filled with all three dimensions of grace. Each prompting of prevenient grace leads to new gifts of forgiveness and acceptance; every growth toward holiness or perfection drives us to deeper dimensions of God's love. By grace we have been saved! By grace we are being saved! By grace we shall be saved to the utmost!

Opportunities for Reflection

The following questions may be used by groups wishing to discuss the material in Chapter Six or by individuals wanting to reflect on issues raised within the chapter.

1. "Grace pervades our understanding of Christian faith and life," affirms *The Book of Discipline*. Do you see this emphasis in your local congregation? The denomination? Share examples.

2. How would you describe the role that grace plays in your life?

3. In what ways does our society value works rather than grace?

4. What are the implications of God's grace for our involvement in such issues as prison reform, economic justice, welfare reform, etc?

Chapter Seven

Accountable Discipleship

From his childhood years in an Anglican rectory until his death at the age of eighty-eight, John Wesley's life was characterized by personal discipline as a means of and response to grace. The disciplined pursuit of "holiness of heart and life"[1] accounts for the name "Methodist" being attached to Wesley and his followers. Although Wesley never particularly liked the term, it describes an important dimension of the Wesleyan understanding of Christian discipleship. The term was first used disparagingly by opponents of Wesley and his colleagues; however, it did express the emphasis that discipleship involves methodical, persistent, disciplined, and accountable obedience.

Living in Response to Grace

While at Oxford University Wesley was involved with a group of persons who shared his commitment to disciplined Christian living. The group was referred to as the Oxford Methodists or the Holy Club. In addition to devoting themselves to study, prayer, self-examination, and mutual admonition, they visited prisons twice each week, spent an hour or two every week in visiting the sick, and regularly ministered to and with the poor. They resolved to do good to as many persons as possible and to refrain from all forms of sin. Although Wesley's motive for such rigorous pursuit of holiness changed from an effort to *earn* God's love and forgiveness to *living in response* to God's grace, obedience and discipline remained an integral part of the Methodist understanding and practice of discipleship.

Living our identity as children of God, and growing toward perfection in love involves keeping covenant with God. The response to Jesus' invitation, "Follow me," (Matthew 4:19) begins a lifelong relationship of obedience and covenant faithfulness. Maintaining the marriage covenant requires sensitive and loving deeds as well as avoiding the temptations to unfaithfulness. Maintaining covenant with Jesus Christ requires acts of devotion in addition to avoiding known sin.

Ours is an age that places emphasis upon feelings—subjectivity—especially in matters pertaining to religion and morality. Relationships, including with God, are judged primarily by the feelings they generate. Love is defined as feelings, being "turned on." The validity and authenticity of religion and religious experience are determined by the intensity of one's feelings. As one person said, "If you don't feel forgiven and saved, you aren't." Faith is interpreted by some as positive assurance or the absence of doubt. Feelings of certainty, optimism, excitement, or serenity become the goals of religious devotion or spiritual quest.

While valuing and affirming feelings and emotions, Methodism has never defined Christian discipleship as subjective feeling. Being Christian is being conformed into the likeness of Jesus Christ. It is exhibiting the fruits of the Spirit, nothing less than holiness of heart and life, being made perfect in love. *Discipleship in the Methodist tradition involves discipline and accountability.*

Faith and Obedience

The Book of Discipline states: "We see God's grace and human activity working together in the relationship of faith and good works. God's grace calls forth human response and discipline. Faith is the only response essential for salvation. However . . . salvation evidences itself in good works."[2] It further affirms, "The coherence of faith with ministries of love forms the discipline of Wesleyan spirituality and Christian discipleship."[3] The doctrinal standards in the United Methodist tradition confess good works as the fruits and manifestations of vital faith.

Methodism has always challenged those who would separate faith from obedience, or faith from works. In Wesley's own time, some religious groups believed that acts of obedience prior to a sense of personal assurance of salvation were "but splendid sins."[4] They believed that one could only wait quietly for a "religious experience" and then obedience would be possible. Wesley strongly disagreed with such a position. He urged the Methodists to trample "under foot that enthusiastic doctrine that 'we are not to do good unless *our hearts be free to it.*'"[5]

Wesley's conviction of the inseparability of faith and obedience grew out of his own experience. Prior to his experience of justification at Aldersgate Street, Wesley had concluded that he should cease preaching. He lacked a sense of assurance. He declared to the Moravian, Peter Böhler, that he had no faith. Wesley's inclusion in his *Journal* of Böhler's response is indicative of its importance in his faith journey: "Preach faith *till* you have it, and then, *because* you have it, you *will* preach faith."[6] As Wesley followed Böhler's advice, his faith and assurance increased. He became convinced that there are degrees of faith; and increased obedience leads to growth in faith.

Obedience does not earn us forgiveness and reconciliation with God; but obedience is necessary to maintain the relationship with God. Married couples may contend that *love* is necessary in order for them to remain faithful to one another. It is even more true that *faithfulness* to one another is necessary in order to keep love alive and growing. An *assurance of God's love and forgiveness* is the ground of Christian discipleship; but *obedience to Jesus Christ* is necessary in order for the ground to produce a harvest.

Faith is acting on the basis of what God has done in Jesus Christ. It is being faithful to the promises and commands of Christ, regardless of feelings and consequences. Faith is obeying Christ's teachings and following Christ's example, trusting that the Holy Spirit will guide and empower us each step of the way. With each act of obedience, faith is strengthened and additional guidance is given. Passively waiting for divine guidance and personal assurance is not faith in the Methodist understanding. Acting in accordance with the teachings and example of Jesus Christ both produces and manifests faith.

For United Methodists, the Christian life is an ongoing,

dynamic pilgrimage toward total restoration of the divine image. It is the endless journey into holiness or perfect love. The journey involves following the commands of God, receiving forgiveness and restoration for failing to follow, and—out of gratitude for the forgiveness and restoration—striving all the more to be obedient.

General Rules for Christian Disciples

Obedience requires understanding who Jesus Christ is and following him. We have to admit that some terrible things are done in the name of obedience to Jesus Christ. History is replete with examples of misdirected obedience—children sacrificed, mass suicides, racial hatred and violence, religious intolerance and persecution, psychological repression, physical abuse, to name but a few. Christ's name has been invoked on behalf of causes which the Jesus Christ witnessed to in Scripture would never sanction. It is important, therefore, that guidelines for obedience to Christ be followed.

For United Methodists the basic guideline is love for God and neighbor. The heart of the Christian way of life, according to John Wesley, is comprised in the Sermon on the Mount. The standard is always conformity to the image of Christ, who is the incarnation of perfect love. Inward holiness (*our love for God*) prompts outward holiness (*our love of neighbor*). Faith active in love is the essence of Christian living.

The pattern for Christian living in the Methodist tradition is set forth in the General Rules for the United Societies. The only requirement for admission in the societies, as noted previously, was "a desire to flee from the wrath to come, and to be saved from their sins." However, continuation in the societies required that the members demonstrate their desire for salvation "*First*, by doing no harm, by avoiding evil of every kind . . . *Secondly*, By doing good; by being in every kind merciful after their power; as they have opportunity, doing good of every possible sort, and, as far as possible, to all men . . . *Thirdly*, By attending upon all the ordinances of God."[7]

Early Methodists believed that these General Rules provided a basic pattern for Christian discipleship. Following Christ

includes avoiding evil and doing no harm. Wesley's list of evil
and harm to be avoided included taking the Lord's name in vain,
profaning the Lord's day, drunkenness, slaveholding, fighting
and quarreling, dishonest advertising, wealthy display, charging
high interest, violating the "Golden Rule," doing anything that
does not "glorify God." The list may need to be updated by contemporary United Methodists, but discipleship would increase if
the spiritual descendants of 'the people called Methodists'
methodically sought to do no harm and to avoid evil of every
kind.

The Importance of "Doing Good"

Following Jesus Christ involves doing good to all persons.
Early Methodists interpreted "doing good" as including ministry
to the physical, spiritual, economic, and mental needs of persons.
Visiting the sick and imprisoned, assisting the poor, providing
employment and medical care, and enduring persecution for the
gospel's sake were but some of the ways the Methodists were to
do good. Social service ministries, education, health care,
involvement in economic issues, aid to the poor, visitation of the
sick and those in prison are but a few of the means by which
United Methodist continue to practice their faith. Obedience to
Jesus Christ means to serve as he served, knowing that " . . .
just as you did it to one of the least of these . . . you did it to"
him (Matthew 25:40).

Wesley considered visitation of and friendship with the poor
as requirements of Christian discipleship and necessary spiritual
disciplines. He viewed relationships with the poor, the sick, and
the imprisoned as indispensable to spiritual maturity. The rationale for such relationships is twofold:

> **First,** obedience to Jesus requires ministry with
> the marginalized, especially the poor.

> **Secondly,** the weak and vulnerable are means of
> grace.

> Since God is especially present among the suffering and the
> vulnerable, we experience God's presence and grace as we share

friendship and aid with the marginalized. Wesley was convinced that authentic religion goes from the weak to the powerful rather than from the powerful to the weak. Otherwise we assume that salvation results from our own power and ingenuity. We cannot share communion with God and fulfill the divine image apart from sharing the life of the poor and the vulnerable.

Faithful discipleship includes "attending upon all the ordinances of God." The early Methodists identified the ordinances as follows:

- The public worship of God
- The ministry of the Word, either read or expounded
- The Supper of the Lord
- Family and private prayer
- Searching the Scriptures
- Fasting or abstinence[8]

More will be said about these ordinances in the next chapter as we focus on means of grace. Growing in faith requires the nurturing of our spiritual lives through worship, participation in the Sacraments, prayer, Bible study, and spiritual disciplines such as fasting.

Moral and ethical integrity, service to others, and spiritual formation are general rules of Christian discipleship. Faith includes obedience to Jesus Christ—acts of compassion and justice as well as acts of personal devotion and worship. Faith and obedience involve self-discipline and individual effort. *Accountability* is also a necessary ingredient of Christian discipleship.

Being Held and Being Held Accountable

Discipleship in the Wesleyan tradition includes *accountability.* The center of early Methodist life were the societies and the class meetings. Methodists were held accountable for their discipleship primarily in the class meetings. The underlying purpose of the class meetings was "to watch over one another in love."[9] In the weekly gatherings, as Wesley said, "a more full inquiry was made into the behaviour of every person . . . advice or reproof was given as need required, quarrels made up, misunderstandings removed; and after an hour or two spent in this labour of love, they concluded with prayer and thanksgiving."[10] In the bands, which consisted of those people who had 'justifying grace', participants were expected to share their struggles in order to be obedient. The following questions were asked in the weekly band meetings:

1. *What known sins have you committed since our last meeting?*
2. *What temptations have you met with?*
3. *How were you delivered?*
4. *What have you thought, said, or done, of which you doubt whether it be sin or not?*
5. *Have you nothing you desire to keep secret?*[11]

Accountability has traditionally been a hallmark of discipleship among United Methodists. However, individualism and personal freedom have eroded accountability and discipline among United Methodists. Individualism makes personal preferences, individual feelings and needs the foundation or criteria for values and behavior. Discipleship is reduced to following one's own conscience, with little reference to accountability to the larger community of faith.

Although Methodists have historically affirmed that the conscience is an arena of God's prevenient grace, we have also recognized that the conscience is shaped and influenced by culture. The conscience drives us to seek what is right, but the definition of what is right varies according to external influences. *"Let your conscience be your guide" is woefully inadequate as the foundation for discipleship unless the conscience has been shaped by Jesus Christ.* Individualism resists accountability to anyone or anything beyond one's own preferences and inclinations. The result is a moral and ethical relativism as well as loss of corporate responsibility.

Christian Freedom

The emphasis upon individual freedom has contributed to diminishing accountability. Freedom of conscience has come to mean the liberty to follow one's own preferences without regard to others. Some interpretations of grace have led to what one the-ologian calls "cheap grace."[12] It is forgiveness without repen-tance, promise without demands, and acceptance understood as indulgence. Freedom is defined as the ability to pursue multiple options without impunity.

Individual freedom has always been an important value among 'the people called Methodist.' Indeed, in Christ we have been set free; but it is a freedom different from license to pursue unlimited options. As Paul writes to the Galatians, "For freedom Christ has set us free . . . For you were called to freedom, broth-ers and sisters; only do not use your freedom as an opportunity for self-indulgence, but through love become slaves to one another" (5:1, 13). Christian freedom includes avoiding such things as "fornication, impurity, licentiousness, idolatry, sorcery, enmities, strife, jealousy, anger, quarrels, dissensions, factions, envy, drunkenness, carousing . . . " (Galatians 5:19-21). Freedom is yoking ourselves to Christ so that the Holy Spirit produces in us such fruits as "love, joy, peace, patience, kindness, generosity, faithfulness, gentleness, and self-control" (Galatians 5:22-23).

Discipleship in the Methodist understanding is a craft requiring persistent use and practice. A craft is learned through apprenticeship and developed through constant use. No one is "free" to be a craftsperson who is unwilling to pay the price to master the necessary skills. A "love for" the craft is a prerequi-site but being a craftsperson involves disciplined and persistent following of guidelines, rules, and principles. The craft of Christian discipleship includes a love for the one the disciples called "Master," a willingness to follow the rules and guidelines set forth in the teachings and example of Christ, and relation-ships in which we are held accountable for living our beliefs.

Christian discipleship requires being held in love and being held accountable. We simply cannot follow Christ apart from a community that holds us in compassion and calls us to account-ability. Solitary discipleship is a misnomer. We cannot be Christian alone. Only with the support, correction, and help of other disciples can we follow Christ. Charles Wesley's hymn expresses the need for supportive and accountable community:

Help us to help each other,
    Lord each other's cross to bear;
let all their friendly aid afford,
    and feel each other's care.
Up unto thee, our living Head,
    let us in all things grow;
till thou hast made us free indeed,
    and spotless here below.
Touched by the lodestone of thy love,
    let all our hearts agree,
and ever toward each other move,
    and ever move toward thee.
To thee, inseparably joined,
    let all our spirits cleave;
O may we all the loving mind
    that was in thee receive.[13]

Conclusion

Christian discipleship is a journey toward maturity in Christ, requiring a lifetime of discipline and accountability. The traditional Methodist emphasis upon accountable obedience has waned in recent years. Rather than conforming to the image of Christ, we have conformed to the individualism and libertinism of the prevailing culture.

Early Methodists represented an alternative way of life to the self-indulgence, hedonism, and social fragmentation of their society. Alternatives to the narcissism, consumerism, and hedonism of contemporary living is desperately needed. Discipleship characterized by being held in love and being held accountable is the means to authentic freedom. In Jesus Christ, God has held us in love; in Jesus Christ we are called into a covenantal relationship; and through the Holy Spirit at work in community we are given power to live in obedience.

Methodists traditionally have participated in an annual Covenant Service. The prayer used in that service proclaims the life of discipleship to which the "people called Methodist" aspire:

I am no longer my own, but thine.
Put me to what thou wilt, rank me with whom
    thou wilt.
Put me to doing, put me to suffering.
Let me be employed by thee or laid aside for
    thee, exalted for thee or brought low by thee.
Let me be full, let me be empty.
Let me have all things, let me have nothing.
I freely and heartily yield all things
    to thy pleasure and disposal.
And now, O glorious and blessed God,
Father, Son, and Holy Spirit,
    thou art mine, and I am thine. So be it.
And the covenant which I have made on earth,
    let it be ratified in heaven. Amen.[14]

Opportunities for Reflection

The following questions may be used by groups wishing to discuss the material in Chapter Seven or by individuals wanting to reflect on issues raised within the chapter.

1. How do you respond to the statement raised in this chapter: "If you don't feel forgiven and saved, you aren't"?

2. The author states that obedience is necessary to maintain a relationship with God. How do you see this in your own life?

3. The author reminds us that Wesley stressed the importance of "doing good" to all persons. How is this emphasis experienced in your life? The life of your congregation?

4. Do you agree with the statement that God is especially present among the suffering and vulnerable? Share your reasons. If you do agree, how can The United Methodist Church enlarge its participation with the poor or marginalized?

Chapter Eight

Means of Grace—Food for the Journey

Sharing God's life and mission through Christian discipleship is a journey toward perfection in love or "holiness of heart and life." Growing in the image of Christ requires faith manifested and strengthened in obedience. Jesus' command, "Come, follow me," is an invitation to share in a transforming friendship with Jesus Christ and an unending pilgrimage toward the kingdom of God, the reign of righteousness. Following Christ is often dangerous, exhausting, and costly. The journey takes us through wildernesses of temptation, valleys of suffering and need, mountain peaks of lofty visions, gardens of anguish, hillsides of crucifixion, and tombs of death and grief.

The demands of discipleship are great, and they cannot be met in our own strength. The good news is that the One who invites us on the journey accompanies us and supplies our needs. The God who liberates people and gives them a new future enables them to live toward their new destiny. God freed the Hebrew people, shaped them into a new people, and led them through the desert into the Promised Land. The God who commanded the people to move forward went before them and provided food for their journey. The law given to Moses, the tabernacle which went before the people, the manna in the wilderness, and leaders such as Moses and Miriam were all means of grace or resources for the journey.

In Jesus Christ, we have been set free from bondage to sin and incorporated into Christ's coming reign over all creation. Christ has invited us to share in the new world of righteousness,

God's victory over evil and death. We have been sent on our way to a new destiny, the kingdom of God. Living toward that new future requires resources we do not have within ourselves. *The One who calls us, however, is the one who provides food for the journey.*

Discipleship in the United Methodist tradition is a process of growth in faith and obedience. Growth requires nourishment and exercise. The General Rules of the Societies and the accountability experienced in the class meetings and bands provided nourishment for those seeking to grow in their discipleship. Methodists since their beginning have identified "the ordinances of God" as *means of grace*—means of God's presence and power. Attendance upon the ordinances of God was required for continued membership in the early Methodist societies because they provided indispensable food for the pilgrimage toward personal and social holiness.

The following are traditional means of grace—*food for the journey*—for United Methodists:

- Public Worship
- Prayer
- Searching the Scriptures
- The Lord's Supper
- Fasting
- Christian Conference

As noted in the previous chapter, avoiding evil and doing works of mercy and justice—especially ministry with the poor— are also means of grace. Obedience is in response to sharing in God's life and mission in Jesus Christ, *not* the precondition for salvation. The ordinances of the church are, therefore, to be seen as gifts of nourishment for disciples on their way to the new heaven and new earth.

Public Worship

The following is a confession in our doctrinal standards:

> *We believe divine worship is the duty and privilege of man [humanity] who, in the presence of*

God, bows in adoration, humility and dedica-
tion. We believe divine worship is essential to
the life of the Church, and that the assembling of
the people of God for such worship is necessary
to Christian fellowship and spiritual growth.[1]

Methodism was nurtured in the rich liturgical life of the
Anglican Church. Although the Methodist movement was cen-
tered in the class meetings and in the open fields where the
masses heard preached the gospel of prevenient, justifying, and
sanctifying grace, worship in the parish church was expected.
Gathering regularly to share praise, confession, the Lord's
Supper, and the Word read and proclaimed was considered foun-
dational for Christian discipleship.

Worship literally means "to declare worth." In worship we
declare the worth of God through acts of praise, confession, lis-
tening, and giving. The focus of worship is the reality and presence of God, not our own needs or desires. Worship differs from
entertainment in that God is the audience and we are the actors.
Our music, prayers, attentiveness, and dedication are gifts we
bring to the transcendent God who graciously enters into communion with us. We hold our lives alongside the holy, righteous,
and loving God. In the presence of the One who is love and holiness, we are "lost in wonder, love and praise."[2] We also are
aware of our failure in love and holiness and seek divine forgiveness. In response to God's presence and forgiveness, we lis-
ten for God's Word and commit ourselves to it. In this regular
rehearsal of our relationship with God in Christ, windows into
grace are opened to us and we are fed by the living Christ
through the Holy Spirit.

Worship is a corporate act. We gather as "the body of
Christ" and by our presence together we affirm that the risen
Christ is with us. Rather than gathering as an audience to individually enjoy or critique the performance, we come together to
jointly share in God's joy and God's critique of us. We help one
another praise, confess, affirm faith, receive the divine Word,
and offer commitments. Therefore, worship is not judged by
"what I get out of it" or the "friendliness of the people."

Worship's effectiveness is judged by the integrity of what the gathered community offers to God.

The form of worship services varies among United Methodists. The style of the music, order of the service, and degree of formality depend upon the cultural context and traditions of the community. The basic pattern of worship, however, includes the following:

- Gathering in the Lord's name through prayer and praise
- Proclamation and Response
- Thanksgiving and Communion (frequency of Holy Communion determined locally)
- Sending Forth into the world.

We are shaped by whatever we consider worthy of praise, confession, and imitation. Gathering in the name and presence of the risen Christ, expressing our praise and confession to the holy and loving God, hearing the Word proclaimed and responding to it, and sharing thanksgiving and communion with one another and Jesus Christ, are means by which the Holy Spirit enables us to grow toward the image of God. *Public worship is food for the journey, a means of God's grace.*

The Sacraments

The Book of Discipline states, "Sacraments ordained of Christ are not only badges or tokens of Christian men's profession, but rather they are certain signs of grace, and God's good will toward us, by which he doth work invisibly in us, and doth not only quicken, but also strengthen and confirm, our faith in him."[3] The Sacraments are acts initiated by Christ as special means of grace by which we share Christ's life, death, resurrection, and final victory. United Methodists acknowledge two Sacraments: Baptism and "the Supper of the Lord."

Baptism

Baptism is initiation into the family of God, cleansing from sin, a sign of new birth as children of God, and empowerment by the Holy Spirit for mission in the world. Our doctrinal standards include this affirmation: "We believe Baptism signifies entrance into the household of faith, and is a symbol of repentance and inner cleansing from sin, a representation of the new birth in Christ Jesus and a mark of Christian discipleship."[4]

Baptism is the means by which we are marked as sons and daughters of God and incorporated into the household of God. It is a declaration of God's *initiative* in claiming and redeeming us. *Baptism celebrates what God has done, is doing, and shall do on our behalf.* It is entrance into Christ's community, the Church; therefore, the community shares in covenant with each baptized person. Since baptism represents God's initiative in claiming, redeeming, and incorporating us into the Christian community, rebaptism and private baptisms are inappropriate.

"We believe children are under the atonement of Christ and as heirs of the Kingdom of God are acceptable subjects for Christian baptism."[5] Our identity as children of God and members of Christ's community and God's forgiving and reconciling action in Jesus Christ are not age related. Therefore, *United Methodists baptize infants and persons of all ages.* The baptism of infants especially affirms God's claim upon us prior to our own response. The baptism of infants is not to be confused with "christening," the giving of a name, or "a dedication" by the parents. *Infant baptism means the same as adult baptism.* In all baptisms the community—the church—promises to nurture and support the baptized in living their God-given identity.

United Methodists consider three modes of baptism equally valid:

1. Sprinkling
2. Pouring
3. Immersion

The three modes have been practiced throughout church history. They carry the same meaning but with special emphases. *Sprinkling* places an emphasis on cleansing; *pouring* reminds us of the bestowing of the Holy Spirit; and *immersion* signifies the burial of the old self and the rising of the new. Cleansing from sin, the pouring upon us of the Holy Spirit, and the gift of new life are dimensions of baptism whatever the mode used. Baptism is a gift of God by which we are born into a new identity, a new community, and a new destiny.

Holy Communion

The Lord's Supper (Holy Communion, or the Eucharist) is "a representation of our redemption, a memorial of the sufferings and death of Christ, and a token of love and union which Christians have with Christ and with one another."[6] It is a participation in the life, death, and resurrection of Jesus Christ and an anticipation of Christ's final victory over sin and death. In remembering Jesus—his birth, life, teachings, death, and resurrection—and in partaking of symbols of his broken body and shed blood, the crucified, risen, and glorified Christ is present with us.

In Holy Communion we share our oneness with Christ, with one another, and with the Christians who have gone before us. We declare, "Because there is one loaf, we, who are many, are one body, for we all partake of the one loaf. The bread which we break is a sharing in the body of Christ. The cup over which we give thanks is a sharing in the blood of Christ."[7] Because the supper is Christ's Supper and not our own, all are invited to share in it. The Invitation affirms: "Christ our Lord invites to his table all who love him, and earnestly repent of their sin and seek to live in peace with one another."[8]

John Wesley urged Methodists to share in the Lord's Supper at least weekly. He believed that regular sharing in the Supper of the Lord provided indispensable nourishment for the soul. Few United Methodists celebrate Holy Communion weekly, although a growing number of churches offer the sacrament every Sunday. Some people hesitate to participate in the sacrament because they "feel unworthy." The feeling of unworthiness is all the more reason to participate, for Holy Communion is the celebration of God's action in making us worthy. The broken bread and shared cup are foretastes of the food we shall share in the heavenly banquet to which we have all been invited.

Acts of Personal Devotion

In addition to public worship and the sacraments, acts of personal devotion are means of grace in the Wesleyan tradition. Private and public prayer, searching the scriptures, and fasting are important avenues of growth in discipleship and expressions of faithfulness to Christ. Through such disciplines, we hold our lives in the presence of God and receive guidance and strength for our walk with Christ in the world. They are means by which we cultivate friendship with Christ, grow toward Christ's likeness, and serve Christ in the world.

Private and Public Prayer

Methodism was born and nurtured in the discipline of *private and public prayer.* Throughout his life, John Wesley followed a strict regimen of daily prayer. His day began and ended with prayer; every hour included pause for prayers of thanksgiving. Other than the Bible, the Anglican *Book of Common Prayer* was the book most used by Wesley. He regularly participated in the Services of Morning and Evening Prayers and many of the prayers of the church had been committed to memory. Prayer was an integral part of every meeting of the societies and classes. He proclaimed in his sermon, *"The Means of Grace," "*. . . all who desire the grace of God are to wait for it in the way of *prayer*. This is the express direction of our Lord himself."[9]

Prayer is communion with God, practicing the presence of God. Through focusing our thoughts upon God, expressing our feelings and dreams and needs to God, and seeking guidance, the transcendent One becomes the immanent One, the holy other becomes a holy presence. Traditional forms of prayer include thanksgiving and praise, petition, and confession. Expressing gratitude and adoration to God lifts us toward transcendent beauty, truth, goodness, and love. Petitions and intercessions are resources which God uses in God's own time and way for the advancement of the divine kingdom. Through confession we admit our sin, request forgiveness, and accept assurance of divine forgiveness. Prayer, therefore, is as indispensable for spiritual health as regular meals are for physical health.

Searching the Scriptures

Searching the Scriptures is a means by which God's grace guides, shapes, and directs us. Our doctrinal standards include the following affirmation of the central role the Bible plays in our discipleship:

> *We believe the Holy Bible, Old and New*
> *Testaments, reveals the Word of God so far as it*
> *is necessary for our salvation. It is to be*
> *received through the Holy Spirit as the true rule*
> *and guide for faith and practice. Whatever is not*
> *revealed in or established by the Holy Scriptures*
> *is not to be made an article of faith nor is it to*
> *be taught as essential to salvation.*[10]

Sharing in God's life and mission involves an understanding of the divine nature and will. Being shaped by God's nature and purpose requires constant, disciplined exposure to God's self-disclosure. The Bible bears witness to God's being and action. It is the story of God's relationship with creation and God's initiatives in seeking to bring to completion the divine purpose of all existence.

The Bible is more than a road map to God's new heaven and new earth. It is a means of divine presence as we journey toward God's vision for all creation. By searching the Scriptures, learning the stories of faith, struggling with their meaning, looking for a Word from the Lord, God comes walking from the pages of the Bible and into our mind and spirit. Through its varied kinds of literature and multiple historical and cultural contexts, the Bible communicates the eternal Word for our time.

John Wesley referred to himself as *homo unius libri*—a man of "one book."[11] He was so familiar with the Bible that its stories, images and expressions were like a second language. He spent time every day in prayerful study of the Scriptures and expected Methodist preachers and class leaders to do the same. His *Explanatory Notes Upon the New Testament* became required reading for early Methodist leaders. It remains one of the means of establishing United Methodist doctrine.

Searching the Scriptures is a personal and communal discipline. Reading the Bible is a personal act in which we engage prayerfully and with openness to the Holy Spirit. Individual study of the Scriptures, utilizing interpretative tools such as commentaries, is a means of growth in discipleship. However, the Bible is the church's book and it is to be read in community. The early Methodist classes and societies devoted time to searching the Scriptures and grappling with their implications. Contemporary United Methodists rediscover the value of studying the Scriptures in community as Disciple Bible Study classes, Sunday school groups, and other settings provide opportunities to explore with other disciples the divine Word found in the Holy Scriptures. Such groups provide both support for continuing exploration and accountability. Reading the Bible in community helps to avoid an individualistic interpretation which ignores its historic message and distorts its meaning.

Fasting

Fasting was considered by the early Methodists as a means of grace. Friday was set aside as a day of fasting. John Wesley wrote: "Is not the neglect of this plain duty (I mean fasting, ranked by our Lord with thanksgiving and prayer) one general occasion of deadness among Christians? Can anyone willingly neglect it and be guiltless?"[12] Fasting was for John Wesley an act of obedience as well as an expression of openness to the divine presence.

Fasting has a long and noble tradition as a means of spiritual devotion. Jesus opened his ministry with a forty-day fast corresponding to that of Moses (Matthew 4:2). He taught that fasting is service to God and a sign of true conversion to the kingdom of God (Matthew 9:14-17). In the Bible, fasting is often connected with prayer. It is a sign of repentance, mourning, and preparation for God's coming. *Abstaining from food serves as a reminder of life's emptiness apart from God's presence and love and our dependence upon divine grace.*

Few modern United Methodists practice fasting and abstinence as a spiritual discipline. Some engage in the discipline occasionally, perhaps during Lent. However, as an act of obedience or an expression of openness to the coming reign of God, fasting can deepen our relationship with Christ and remind us of Christ's presence with impoverished and suffering people. Following the example and teaching of Jesus, fasting becomes a means of anticipating the heavenly banquet when Christ's reign of generosity and joy comes to completion.

Christian Conference

Another traditional Methodist means of grace is *Christian Conference,* or "right conversation." The early Methodists gathered regularly to discuss important theological concepts and missional strategies. Wesley considered such conferences as indispensable means of discerning God's will and sharing in God's mission in the world. Although the first Methodist conferences included only the leaders of the movement, meeting together for conversation with other Methodists to share issues of faith and mission became a distinguishing mark of Methodism's connectional life.

The modern *charge conference* and *annual conference* have their origins in the understanding that conferencing is a means of grace. In more recent years, however, United Methodist conferences have become more focused on administrative and business issues than on theological reflection, missional strategy, or spiritual discernment. They tend to be dominated by parliamentary procedure, committee reports, and organizational functions. The loss of the original intent of conferences has contributed to a blurring of theological vision and a weakening of missional power.

Conversation with other Christians around issues of faith and mission is a means by which God guides and strengthens us. Sharing our understandings and struggles with others who are seeking to participate in God's life and work opens new avenues of divine grace and guidance. Through such sharing, the Holy Spirit is present to direct, empower, and transform. Dialogue in an atmosphere of humility and respect is a form of evangelism and prophetic witness. Jesus promised, "For where two or three are gathered in my name, I am there among them" (Matthew 18:20). In the midst of honest discussion and through the power of the Holy Spirit, the risen Christ comes to provide food for our journey toward the fulfillment of God's purpose.

Conclusion

Living as disciples of Jesus Christ is an unending journey. Holiness of heart and life, being made perfect in love, and being a citizen of God's new heaven and new earth involves far more than a one-time experience of divine forgiveness. Salvation, the complete restoration of the divine image in us and in all creation, is a continuing process. Following Jesus Christ inevitably puts us at odds with the world as it is, and the struggle is both internal and external. Sin continues to stalk us and temptation never forsakes us. Principalities and powers in the form of political and economic realities and cultural expectations and practices constantly lure us away from loyalty to Christ. Sharing in the life of the world, as it is, is easier than sharing in the life and work of God's world of justice, righteousness, generosity, and joy.

The God who calls us out of bondage and into a new world does not leave us alone in the wilderness. As God gave manna in the wilderness to the Hebrew slaves en route to the promised land, God provides food for our journey toward a world transformed by Jesus Christ. Friendship with the One who goes before us is our nourishment and the source of our guidance. Friendship is nurtured by and expressed in obedience kept alive through means of grace.

Public worship, participation in the Sacraments, private and public prayer, searching the Scriptures, fasting, and Christian conferences are acts of devotion in the Wesleyan tradition. They are not forms of works righteousness by which we earn a relationship with Christ. They are gifts by which our lives are shaped by friendship with Christ. Through them, we express our devotion and open our lives to the presence and power of God. They become means by which we are fed the Bread of Life, which nourishes our souls unto everlasting life.

Opportunities for Reflection

The following questions may be used by groups wishing to discuss the material in Chapter Eight or by individuals wanting to reflect on issues raised within the chapter.

1. As you consider the acts of devotion mentioned in this chapter, which acts have most meaning for you? Most challenge? Why?

2. If charge conferences or annual conferences focused less on administrative/business issues and more on spiritual discernment or theological reflection, how might The United Methodist Church be affected?

3. In what ways are the spiritual disciplines (acts) discussed in this chapter really "food for the journey"?

Chapter Nine

Church: A Called and Committed People

John Wesley wrote in 1785: "How much do we almost continually hear about the Church! . . . And yet how few understand what they talk of! How few know what the term means! A more ambiguous word than this, the 'church,' is scarce to be found in the English language."[1] Today in America, churches exist in almost every neighborhood. A majority of people count themselves as church members. Yet, confusion abounds as to the nature and purpose of the church, even among those who participate regularly in its activities.

Critics contend that the church has lost its identity and reason for existence. What difference does the church make? How different, if any, would neighborhoods be if churches were not present? Disturbing studies indicate that people who belong to churches reflect the values, attitudes, and behavior of the society. Once the church was a major moral and ethical influence in society; now, however, its voice on the issues of private and public morality has been marginalized or confined to a narrow political agenda.

Walter Brueggemann in his book, *Biblical Perspectives on Evangelism,* diagnoses the contemporary church's problem as "amnesia."[2] The influential scholar contends that the church has lost its memory. It has forgotten what and whose it is. As a person with amnesia depends upon other people to define who he/she is, the church that does not know its own origin and destiny receives its identity from the world around it. Without a memory of what the church is *called* to be, the church becomes what people *want* it to be. The self-defined needs and wishes of the people become more influential than God's mission to the world. Sociological surveys, marketing strategies, and multiple option activities become tools more basic than doctrinal clarity, accountable discipleship, missional focus, and liturgical and theological integrity.

The church is treated as another voluntary organization which people join as they do a civic club or a political party. Loyalty is measured by frequency of attendance, payment of pledges, service on committees, and participation in activities. The church is considered to be something we *belong to* rather than *someone we are*. Membership and participation are viewed as optional, depending upon personal preferences and satisfaction. The church, then, is seen as another institution among many institutions competing for our time, energy, and financial resources. *Its distinctiveness as a called people of God committed to being a sign, foretaste, and instrument of God's presence and power is lost amid institutional survival and personal satisfaction.*

The church's identity and mission are rooted in God. As a community called into being for the purpose of participating in God's life and mission in the world, the church must live its divine identity and mission. The United Methodist Church's distinctive heritage and emphases provide resources for reclaiming and strengthening the church's transforming and redemptive presence in society.

Methodism's Beginnings

Methodism began as a reform and missional movement within the Church of England. John Wesley and the Methodists set out "to reform the nation, particularly the Church, and to spread scriptural holiness over the land."[3] Early Methodists wanted to spread in the hearts of people the love of God, not to establish a new church. Early Methodists continued to participate in the worship and sacramental life of the Anglican Church. Since members of the classes and societies were expected to share in worship of their parish churches, Methodist meetings were scheduled at times other than Sunday mornings. John and

Charles Wesley maintained their status as priests in the Church of England. No Methodist Church was formed in England until after the death of John Wesley.

Methodists first formed themselves into an organized church in America. In 1784 the Methodist Episcopal Church was organized, but the emphasis on evangelization and mission continued to dominate the new church's self-understanding and structure. The basic doctrines were Wesley's adaptation of the Anglican Articles of Religion. American Methodists, like their counterparts in England, were occupied with proclaiming the gospel and forming disciples of Jesus Christ. The circuit riders travelled widely across the frontier and were often the first to greet the new settlers. They provided instruction, inspiration, and the sacraments during their visits in local communities. The center of congregational life remained in the class meetings, preaching houses, and revival meetings. Laity provided basic leadership; class leaders and lay preachers provided ongoing pastoral care in the absence of circuit riders. Organizational structures, buildings, and formalized doctrinal statements were less important than making disciples.

As American society became more organized and bureaucratized, so did the Methodist Church. Eventually the circuit rider became the pastor of the local congregation. Buildings and organization took on added importance as the Methodist Church became the largest Protestant denomination in nineteenth and early twentieth century America. Still, the origins as a reform and missional movement continued to shape the Methodist Church's life and work. Since Methodism did not begin as a result of doctrinal disputes or theological distinctiveness, that which gave the church identity was its mission to "reform the nation and spread scriptural holiness."

The Nature and Mission of the Church

Our doctrinal standards contain the following description of the church's identity and mission:

We believe the Christian Church is the community of all true believers under the Lordship of

Christ. We believe it is one, holy, apostolic and catholic. It is the redemptive fellowship in which the Word of God is preached by men [persons] divinely called, and the sacraments are duly administered according to Christ's own appointment. Under the discipline of the Holy Spirit the Church exists for the maintenance of worship, the edification of believers and the redemption of the world.[4]

The Book of Discipline affirms that " . . . the Holy Spirit calls the church into being as the instrument of the good news of grace to all people." It further states, "A grace-formed church is one which responsibly participates in God's action in and for the world."[5] The church is a people called into being by God to be a sign, foretaste, and instrument of God's victory over the power of sin and death. As the community under the sovereignty of Christ, the church is the body of Christ in the world—an extension of Christ's ministry.

The church's purpose is not its own. The church is to be present in the world on behalf of the God by whose grace it has been called into existence. What is the nature of God's presence in the world? God's presence is creative and redemptive. Where there is chaos, whether in the natural or social realm, God is present to create harmony. Where there is bondage—personal, political, or social—God is active to liberate and free the enslaved. Where there are walls dividing human beings into the privileged and the deprived, God seeks to destroy oppressive divisions through judgment and reconciliation. Where there is despair, loneliness, brokenness, and sickness, God is present to heal and mend. As Jesus Christ came "to bring good news to the poor . . . to proclaim release to the captives and recovery of sight to the blind, to let the oppressed go free, to proclaim the year of the Lord's favor" (Luke 4:18), so the church is to be redemptively present with the poor, the captive, the blind, and the oppressed. It is to announce in word and deed the coming of God's justice and righteousness.

The church exists as an alternative community, a light to the world, a beacon of God's coming Kingdom brought near in Jesus Christ. Its hospitable fellowship with all God's children points toward God's universal love. Its concern for and friendship with the impoverished, the despised and vulnerable people of the world announces God's special presence with the marginalized, the abused, and the outcast. The church's moral integrity and commitment to justice is a prophetic witness to God's holiness and righteousness. The centrality of worship holds before the world the presence of transcendent beauty, goodness, truth, and love. A church shaped by divine grace stands as an alternative to society's reliance on success, prestige, wealth, and power as means of happiness and salvation.

God's redemptive and creative presence is not limited to one denomination. Methodists are part of the church universal. In the Apostles' Creed we affirm our belief in and commitment to "the holy catholic church," God's covenant community which transcends national boundaries, denominational structures, and historical presence. We are part of God's universal and eternal presence and mission. As a member of the body of Christ, The United Methodist Church makes a distinctive contribution to God's universal and timeless mission.

Methodism's Distinctive Contributions to the Universal Church

The United Methodist Church shares with the church universal a common faith in Jesus Christ. We share a common mission to be present in the world as God is present. United Methodism's structure and polity reflect three theological/missional emphases which contribute significantly to the universal church. These emphases are often interpreted administratively and bureaucratically rather than theologically and missionally. However, only by understanding the theological and missional foundation for *connectionalism, itineracy*, and *catholicity* can United Methodism live its identity and fulfill its mission.

Connectionalism

The United Methodist Church is a *connectional* church. Ever since John Wesley referred to Methodist classes, bands and societies scattered throughout eighteenth-century England as "the connexion," the "people called Methodists" have understood themselves as a people of faith who journey together in covenant with God and one another. Our identity is in our wholeness together in Christ. Each part is vital to the whole. *No local congregation, no conference or general church agency functions in isolation.* Every aspect of the church's life functions is an intricate web of interdependency, support, and accountability.

Methodist connectionalism is rooted in the biblical concept of covenant. God entered into covenant with Abraham and Sarah and their descendants. They were to be God's people, a light to all nations. God would be their God and would lead them toward the fulfillment of the divine vision for humanity. As a covenant people, the people of Israel were to obey God's commands, practicing justice and mercy toward one another and all peoples. The twelve tribes of Israel were bound together by their covenant with God and with one another as the people of God.

The United Methodist Church is made up of local congregations, districts, annual conferences, jurisdictional conferences, and the general or global conference. Each component has authority and responsibility; each is related to, dependent upon, and in ministry with the other components. The covenant is expressed through shared missional efforts around the world, shared financial support, appointed pastoral leadership, oversight by bishops and district superintendents, a doctrinal statement, constitution, and structural polity approved by the General Conference. No one person or organization within The United Methodist Church is autonomous. Everyone and all structures are accountable to the whole, reminding us that the final authority is Christ.

Our connectionalism, then, is an expression of our understanding of the church as the body of Christ, with each part of the body having distinctive functions. Yet it is related to and dependent upon the others. Through our connectional relationships we are reminded of our covenant with God which transcends our differences and thereby enables us to maintain unity amid diversity. Through God's grace we are connected with God's own life and we share in fellowship and ministry with diverse peoples throughout the world and throughout history. *Connectionalism is also a missional strategy.* We can do together what no individual, congregation, or conference can do alone. Because of our connectional polity, The United Methodist Church provides a wholistic ministry to the whole world. Through connectional channels, United Methodists have several hundred missionaries in countries throughout the world. Emergency and relief assistance is sent immediately into areas where disasters occur. Education is provided in scores of colleges and universities and seminaries. Curriculum and Bible study materials for all ages and settings are produced. Leadership training and resources are provided. Neighborhood centers, hospitals, retirement and nursing homes, child care programs and institutions, and urban and rural mission centers minister to thousands of people in the name of Christ. As people in covenant with God and one another, The United Methodist Church seeks to embody the central affirmation expressed by the Apostle Paul: " . . . in Christ God was reconciling the world to himself . . . and entrusting the message of reconciliation to us" (2 Corinthians 5:19).

Itineracy

Itineracy is another distinctive emphasis of Methodism. Clergy have their membership in the annual conference rather than the local church. Clergy are assigned to their areas of ministry by a bishop. Bishops are elected by the jurisdictional conferences and their membership is in the Council of Bishops. Bishops are assigned to conferences by the Jurisdictional Committee on the Episcopacy. All clergy, therefore, hold membership in a body to which they are accountable and they are appointed to their specific area of ministry. They are subject to assignment in accordance with the missional needs of the church.

Itineracy is grounded in two basic theological affirmations—*incarnation* and a *called and sent ministry.* God's presence and truth have become incarnate in Jesus Christ. Jesus is the unique and supreme embodiment of the presence, love, and mission of the eternal God. However, God seeks to incarnate the divine presence, love, and mission in every person. Each person has unique gifts, qualities, and perspectives which God calls forth and uses as means of ministry to the world. Since God's fullness has only been incarnate in one person—Jesus Christ—all others express only partial manifestations of God's presence and ministry. No pastor or lay person can adequately bear witness to the fullness of divine grace. Itinerant ministry affirms that each pastor brings unique gifts and perspectives which over time provides congregations fuller expressions of God's presence and ministry.

John Wesley encountered objections to an itinerant ministry early in the formation of Methodism. Wesley followed the practice of moving preachers first every two years and then mostly every year. The rationale was rooted in Wesley's incarnational understanding of ministry. He wrote: "This [itineracy] has always shown that the people profit less by any one person than by a variety of preachers; while they 'used the gifts on each bestowed, tempered by the act of God.'"[6] Wesley assigned preachers with the assumption that the people benefitted from the variety of gifts that preachers bring to ministry.

Itineracy has also functioned as a counter to "preacher worship." Methodists traditionally have avoided basing their loyalty to the church on a particular pastor. *Pastors are temporary;* our commitment is to Jesus Christ whose ministry transcends the personalities of the pastors. Since no one pastor embodies the fullness of God's grace and mission, the congregation can celebrate the gifts of each pastor; and pastors can affirm the unique gifts and ministries of a variety of congregations.

The history of God's mission to the world has always included the *calling* and *sending* of persons. Itineracy affirms the call and sent nature of ministry. All ministry is participation in God's ministry to and with the world. Laity and clergy share in that called and sent ministry. We are called to be the people of God and sent into the world to bear witness to God's grace-filled action on behalf of the world. Itineracy reminds us, laity and clergy, that we are a pilgrim people who are called out (the *ecclesia)* and sent toward the new heaven and new earth, the kingdom of God. We are not homesteaders; we are sojourners, living temporarily in this world while our citizenship is in another world. We are always under command of Christ who called the disciples and sent them out to proclaim the coming of the kingdom. We are not our own; we have been called, empowered, and sent.

In addition to being an expression of incarnation and a called and sent ministry, itineracy is also a *missional strategy.* John Wesley adopted an itinerant ministry as a means of deploying preachers where they were most needed. Called "traveling preachers," they were expected to move throughout the connection in order to evangelize. Circuit riders were deployed on the American frontier, often arriving in an area with or before the first homesteaders. The ability to deploy leadership quickly and strategically helps to account for the success of the Methodists in evangelization and the planting of new congregations across the American frontier.

Itineracy has changed significantly since Wesley sent preachers across eighteenth century England and into the prisons, slums, and open fields. Itineracy is not the same today as when circuit riders rode into the wilderness of the new world. Longer tenure and consultation are necessary accommodations to the changing needs and dynamics of American culture. However, the theological and missional foundation of itineracy remains a strong witness to the world, provided it is not eroded by a localism which compromises the broader mission and a clergy professionalism that uses itineracy to enhance career advancement or promote personal agendas.

Catholicity

Another distinctive ecclesial emphasis of Methodists is *catholicity,* or unity among God's people. Just as no local congregation or connectional component can be a full expression of the body of Christ, neither can one denomination. God's grace-filled ministry encompasses the full range of denominational structures and polities. Denominational chauvinism and competitiveness are contrary to the Wesleyan tradition. Openness to diversity, tolerance of differences, and ecumenical or cooperative ministries have characterized Methodism since its inception.

Methodism's historic ecumenical emphasis is expressed in Wesley's famous sermon entitled, "Catholic Spirit." He wrote:

> *I dare not therefore presume to impose my mode of worship on any other. I believe it is truly primitive and apostolical. But my belief is no rule for another. I ask not therefore of him with whom I would unite in love, "Are you of my Church? Of my congregation? Do you receive the same form of church government and allow the same church officers with me? Do you join in the same form of prayer wherein I worship God?" I inquire not, "Do you receive the Supper of the Lord in the same posture and manner that I do?" Nor whether, in the administration of baptism, you agree with me in admitting sureties for the baptized, in the manner of administering it, or the age of those to whom it should be administered . . . Let all these things stand by: we will talk of them, if need be, at a more convenient season. My only question at present is this, "Is thine heart right, as my heart is with thy heart?"[7]*

Wesley affirmed that love for God and neighbor is the heart of religion and the catholic (universal) spirit is catholic (universal) love. A characteristic of Methodism throughout its history is this: *In essentials, unity; in nonessentials, liberty; and in all things, charity.*

Catholic spirit and tolerance of differences, however, are not to be interpreted as indifference to sound doctrine. Wesley warned: "Observe this, you who know not what spirit ye are of, who call yourselves men of a catholic spirit only because you are of a muddy understanding; because your mind is all in a mist; because you have not settled, consistent principles, but are for jumbling all opinions together."[8] Methodists affirm the core doctrines of the apostolic faith. Beliefs and doctrines, however, are always subordinate to love for God and neighbor. Doctrinal differences can never be used as rationale for persecuting, hating, or failing to love another.

Since God is the one sovereign of all creation and since the church is called to reflect the image of God, the church has no choice but to exhibit oneness. A dominate biblical image of God's vision for the world is that the human family will be one, that people will come to know themselves as children of God and as brothers and sisters under the parenthood of God. The church is to be shaped by that vision of catholicity or unity. The United Methodist emphasis on catholic spirit summons all to live in union with one another under the sovereignty of God's universal love.

Conclusion

God's preoccupation is the salvation of the world, the reconciliation of all things in Jesus Christ. The church is called to share in God's ministry of salvation and reconciliation. The calling is fulfilled as the people of God live in accordance with God's revelation in Jesus Christ. The church is to embody the power, presence, and love of God and participate in the divine initiative to bring justice, peace, joy, and love to all creation. The church, therefore, is a sign which points to God's presence and purposes. It is a foretaste of God's coming victory already begun in the life, teaching, death, resurrection, and ascension of Jesus Christ. The church is to be an instrument which God uses to bring the kingdom of justice, generosity, and joy.

The church is our identity; it is not an organization to which we belong in accordance with our preferences and convenience. We are a called people, shaped and empowered by the Christ whom we serve. As we live our identity in the home, the school, the neighborhood, the workplace, the political arena, and the institutional church, we share in God's life and mission. We become an alternative community bound together by common loyalty to Jesus Christ.

United Methodism is one manifestation of the universal church. Within the broader church, Methodists offer at least three distinctive ecclesial emphases—*connectionalism, itineracy, and catholicity.* The fragmented, broken world needs the witness of a community connected by a covenant with God and one another. A society which places priority on individualism and "doing my own thing" longs for models of servant leadership reflected in a sense of being called and sent to incarnate the grace of God. When religious differences continue to fuel animosity and violence, a church that emphasizes catholicity or universal love is essential. *The contemporary world needs the witness of The United Methodist Church.*

A hymn by Fred Pratt Green captures the church's identity and challenge:

> *The church of Christ, in every age beset by*
> *   change but Spirit led,*
> *must claim and test its heritage and keep on ris-*
> *   ing from the dead.*
> *Across the world, across the street, the victims*
> *   of injustice cry*
> *for shelter and for bread to eat, and never live*
> *   until they die.*
> *Then let the servant church arise, a caring*
> *   church that longs to be*
> *a partner in Christ's sacrifice, and clothed in*
> *   Christ's humanity.*
> *For he alone, whose blood was shed, can cure*
> *   the fever in our blood,*
> *and teach us how to share our bread and feed*
> *   the starving multitude.*
> *We have no mission but to serve in full obedi-*
> *   ence to our Lord,*
> *to care for all, without reserve, and spread his*
> *   liberating word.[9]*

Opportunities for Reflection

The following questions may be used by groups wishing to discuss the material in Chapter Nine or by individuals wanting to reflect on issues raised within the chapter.

1. As you read this chapter, what do you see to be the unique witness of The United Methodist Church?

2. Methodism began as a reform and missional movement. In what ways might United Methodism continue its historic work?

3. What strengths does connectionalism offer the world? What strengths does catholicity offer? Itineracy?

Chapter Ten

Doctrinal Faithfulness and Continuing Exploration

Sharing the life and mission of God, who transcends human comprehension and whose mission encompasses a new heaven and new earth, involves us in an endless journey. Since God is more than can be totally described in creeds, community with God's life and participating in God's mission requires continuing exploration and persistent openness to new insights and revelations. God's reconciled and redeemed creation is only partially realized in human history; therefore, participating in the divine mission requires an unending effort to discern God's will and a willingness to follow Christ into new arenas of service. Every age presents the people of God with new challenges. The apostolic faith must be interpreted anew to every generation.

The contemporary world presents the Christian faith with particular challenges. The world of the twenty-first century is vastly different from the age of the apostles or the era of John Wesley. Science and technology have altered every aspect of life—our food, clothing, shelter, transportation, communication, medicine, education, entertainment, work. Life and death decisions, once attributed only to God, are now thrust upon us. Places and people—once so distant as to remain unknown—are now within easy reach by telephone, television, and travel. Information, once unavailable or stored in books, is now instantaneously accessible through home computers. Feats that at one time were considered fictional or miraculous are performed daily in hospitals, airports and space launching pads, scientific laboratories, and manufacturing facilities.

Is God a stranger in this new world of science and technology? As one youth asked, "Does God understand nuclear physics and genetics?" The world of space exploration, gene manipulation, computer technology, organ transplants, test tube babies, economic interdependency, and global neighborhoods challenges traditional concepts of God and God's relationship with the world. Without a willingness to engage in serious explorations into God's nature, purpose and presence, the church will answer questions *nobody is asking* and become a monument to a static and distant God.

Methodism affirms the necessity of maintaining the truth of historic apostolic doctrines *and* engaging in continuing explorations into God's life and mission. The tension between holding fast the doctrines and interpreting and applying ancient revelation to new situations is the growing edge of faith and obedience. Sharing the life of a God who is sovereign of the past, present and future demands loyalty to what God has done and openness to what God is doing and shall do.

Exploring New Frontiers of Faith

Remaining faithful to the apostolic faith, while interpreting and applying that faith to contemporary situations, is the task of every Christian. The temptation is to remove the inherent tension of faith by opting either for a dogmatic creedalism or a doctrinal indifferentism. Both rigid dogma and indifference to sound doctrine are contrary to United Methodist tradition and practice. *The Book of Discipline* describes the role of doctrine and theological reflection:

> *While the Church considers its doctrinal affirmations as a central feature of its identity and restricts official changes to a constitutional process, the Church encourages serious reflection across the theological spectrum.*
>
> *As United Methodists, we are called to identify the needs both of individuals and of society and to address those needs out of the resources of*

*Christian faith in a way that is clear, convincing,
and effective. Theology serves the Church by
interpreting the world's needs and challenges to
the Church and by interpreting the gospel to the
world.*[1]

By placing emphasis upon both doctrine and continuing
theological exploration, United Methodists acknowledge that
faith is dynamic, growing, and relevant to changing contexts.
Sharing in God's life and participating in God's mission is more
than mental assent to ancient creeds. It is an endless process of
understanding what God *has done*, discerning what God *is
doing*, and visioning what God *will do*. Faith is acting upon the
truth God has revealed in the historic doctrines and remaining
faithful even when God seems remote or absent. Faithfulness
involves trusting the God made known in Jesus Christ although
the changing world presents new challenges to faith.

The historic doctrines of the church provide a place to stand
amid the shifting sands of turbulent change. They also serve as
home base from which we launch continuing explorations into
God's being and mission. Without historic doctrines, our explorations are without compass and guide. The results are needless
wanderings in the wilderness of confusion, being led astray by
destructive idols, and distorting God's nature and mission.

Doctrines provide a framework and parameters for understanding God and exploring God's nature and purpose. Dr.
Thomas Langford suggests a helpful analogy: "Doctrine is like a
house that a religious communion already inhabits. It represents
a communal agreement about what is essential to and characteristic of their faith."[2] Theological inquiry, on the other hand, "is
the proposal of blueprints for extending the house. Often individually drawn, these blueprints represent creative efforts to sug-
gest new construction which will make the home more welcom-
ing or adequate."[3]

Living in the house of faith and engaging in new construction
require the use of reliable tools. The United Methodist Church
affirms the following as reliable tools for maintaining sound doctrine and engaging in theological reflection and exploration:

- Scripture
- Tradition
- Experience
- Reason

The Centrality of the Bible

The *primary* source and criterion for determining doctrine and engaging in theological exploration is the Bible. The centrality of Scripture in matters of faith is clearly affirmed in The United Methodist standards of doctrine. The Articles of Religion include the following:

> *The Holy Scriptures containeth all things necessary to salvation; so that whatsoever is not read therein, nor may be proved thereby, is not to be required of any man that it should be believed as an article of faith, or be thought requisite or necessary to salvation.*[4]

As stated in a previous chapter, John Wesley referred to himself as "a man of one book." He wrote, "I began not only to read, but to study the Bible, as the one, the only standard of truth, and the only model of pure religion."[5] Albert Outler affirms, "Wesley's point of departure was always Holy Scripture, understood according to the 'analogy of faith' (i.e., its general sense), and as 'the standing revelation' in the Christian Church throughout her long history."[6]

United Methodists believe that the Bible is primary in matters of faith; its authority lies in the Living Word to which the Bible bears witness. It is not the verbal inspiration or factual accuracy that gives the Bible authority. God's revelation, supremely given in Christ, is the Bible's source of authority. The Bible serves for us the role that John the Baptist served for the Messiah. He bore witness to the light but was not to be equated with the light. The Bible points to the One who is life's supreme authority, God made known in Jesus Christ.

United Methodists take the Bible with utmost seriousness even though many do not take it literally. Serious reading of the Bible requires taking its historical and literary setting into consideration. It involves entering the world of the Bible, struggling with its language and symbols, literary devices, and cultural context. Taking the Bible seriously requires that the reader be open to the Holy Spirit who brings the Eternal Word in the midst of the temporal needs of the reader. Reading the Bible in solitude and in community is a means of understanding God and sharing in God's guiding and empowering presence.

The Bible, of course, can be misused. Although the Bible is considered as the *primary* source and criterion for understanding God's revelation, its truths and insights are not self-evident. Scripture does not yield its divine secrets carelessly or casually. Discerning the Eternal Word within the words of the Bible demands hard work and risky struggle. Most Christians need help in using the Bible as a vehicle of God's presence and revelation. Following are a few general guidelines for interpreting Scripture.

A Book of Theology

First, the Bible is to be read and studied primarily as the story about God and God's relationship with creation and human beings. Although it contains history, science, psychology, and various types of literature, the Bible is principally a book of theology, the story of God. It is not meant to be a textbook of science or history. History is recounted not primarily to provide facts about events but to reveal something about God. Facts and details are less important that the deeper truth of God's presence and purposes.

For example, the story of Jonah in the Old Testament does not focus on a fish swallowing a man. Its central revelation is this: God's mercy and love are universal and includes those we may label as enemy. The creation stories in Genesis are not scientific accounts of how creation came into being. They are affirmations that creation and human beings have their origin and existence in God who brings order out of chaos, light out of darkness, life out of nothingness.

Jesus Christ—The Measure of Scripture

Second, each part of the Bible is to be interpreted in terms of the total message of Scripture. Reading passages in isolation from the broader biblical message results in proof-texting and may distort God's revelation. All passages must be interpreted in the light of the life, teachings, death and resurrection of Jesus Christ. That is, Jesus Christ is the measure of the Bible's message. That which contradicts the spirit of Jesus must be treated with suspicion or subordination. For example, a passage such as Psalm 137:9 that extols the slaughter of the enemy's children must be measured against Jesus' treatment of children and his warning to those who would harm them.

Reading Contextually

Third, each book of the Bible must be interpreted first in terms of its historical context. When was it written? Who wrote it? What was the situation the book sought to address? What did it mean to the persons to whom it was written? In order to know what the Bible *means,* we must know what it *meant.* Severing Scripture from its historical context results in manipulating its message to serve the interpreter's purposes. Failing to understand, for example, that the Book of Revelation was written to give encouragement to people being persecuted at the hands of the Roman Emperor can lead to using the book to frighten the faithful or using it as a foretelling of coming historic events.

Fourth, each passage is to be read and interpreted in its literary context. Where is the passage located? What precedes and follows it in the text? What kind of literature is it? Poetry? Prose? Narrative? Letter? Parable? Allegory? Prophecy? Apocalypse? What literary devices are used? Understanding the literary form and context enables the reader to get inside the biblical material and sense its drama and insight. One can identify with the characters in the stories, experience the surroundings, feel the movement, and confront the issues. Reading the Psalms as prayers and hymns, for example, can give expression to our own feelings and needs in the presence of God.

Explore Implications

Fifth, after considering the passage in its broader biblical, historical, and literary context, the interpreter begins to raise questions as to the implications for his or her own life and experience: What are the similarities between the situation addressed in the passage and our own situation? What are the differences? What does the passage say about God, God's presence, or God's purposes in and for our time and my life? What difference would it make if we lived in terms of this passage? What changes would take place? What are the obstacles to living in terms of this passage? Does the Bible offer insight and motivation for removing the obstacles? Can I illustrate the insight of this passage in my own life?

Consult Scholarship

Sixth, the reader may wish to consult what others have said or written about the passage. Numerous commentaries are available which help to understand the historical and literary context and to provide insights others have gleaned from the passage. Sharing insights from and with the church's biblical scholars and students is a means of being held accountable and it makes one less likely to misinterpret and misuse the Bible.

Tradition—Source and Criterion

The Book of Discipline contains this affirmation of the role of tradition in defining doctrine and engaging in theological exploration:

> *The theological task does not start anew in each age or each person. Christianity does not leap from New Testament times to the present as though nothing were to be learned from that great cloud of witnesses in between. For centuries Christians have sought to interpret the truth of the gospel for their time.*[7]

According to the Bible, God speaks and acts in the events of history. The Exodus of the Hebrews from Egyptian slavery,

the giving of the Law on Sinai, the building of the Hebrew
nation, the Assyrian and Babylonian captivity and subsequent
restoration, the Incarnation in Jesus of Nazareth, Pentecost, and
the creation of the church—these are key events in the church's
tradition. The hymns, prayers, affirmations of the Psalms, and
liturgies of Judaism and the early church form part of the store-
house of the church's tradition. The writings of the early church
leaders contain revelatory insights that cannot be ignored by
those who seek to know God in the contemporary world. Neither
can we ignore the historic creeds and the life stories of pilgrims
of faith through the ages. The cumulative experience of our
mothers and fathers in the faith become the story which gives us
identity and vision for the future.

Tradition is multifaceted and diverse. It, too, must be interpreted holistically and in the light of Scripture. Tradition can be
used to justify actions and beliefs that are contrary to Scripture
and the example and spirit of Jesus. Nevertheless, tradition
reflects a continuity of experience and revelation. Ignoring the
continuity of tradition's themes and insights in our continuing
quest is as absurd as attempting to face each new day with no
memory of the past.

John Wesley urged his contemporaries to "acquire a 'knowledge of the Fathers', because they were the most authentic com-
mentators on Scripture, as being both nearest to the fountain, and
eminently endued with that Spirit by whom all Scripture is
given."[8] Wesley was as familiar with the early history of the
church as any person in eighteenth-century England. He could
readily call upon church tradition as a resource for confronting
issues of life and faith. Few United Methodists, however, are
thoroughly acquainted with church traditions. The historic
creeds—such as the Apostles' Creed, the Nicene Creed, and the
Articles of Religion and Confession of Faith in our own *Book of
Discipline*—along with the hymns and liturgies of the church
provide concise summaries and dominate themes of traditional
theological insights and parameters.

Tradition also includes the broader range of human experience. Just as God acts uniquely in *each person*, so God acts
uniquely in *each culture*. Therefore, learning and appreciating

the traditions of other cultures can be a means of deepening our understanding and experience of God. African-Americans, Hispanics, Africans, Asians, Native Americans, Latinos, as well as Europeans comprise the traditions of Methodism. Included in our doctrinal and liturgical heritage are pietism, evangelicalism, revivalism, social action, high liturgy and liturgical spontaneity. All contribute to the ongoing journey toward the fullness of God's presence and revelation.

Experience as a Tool for Knowing God

Experience, like tradition and reason, is both an avenue of God's presence and a tool for discerning God's purposes. Divine grace and presence are known in the midst of life's experiences. There is a transcendent dimension to all experiences as the Holy Spirit works within the routines of living. Growth in discipleship requires a constant openness to the One in whom we live and move and have our being.

The Wesleyan understanding of *experience* is twofold. First, it refers to the personal assurance of God's justifying, pardoning grace. As *The Book of Discipline* affirms: "'New life in Christ' is what we as United Methodists mean when we speak of 'Christian experience.'"[9] All doctrines and theological reflections, according to Methodist tradition, have as their basic purpose and authority the experience of God's prevenient, justifying, and sanctifying grace. A valid question to ask of all doctrines and beliefs is this: *Does it promote or enhance new life in Christ?*

Experience in the Wesleyan understanding also refers to the common-sense experience of the individual and the community. Experiences of the individual and the entire human family are avenues of insight and revelation, as well as criteria by which beliefs are judged. Our life experiences influence how we perceive God, how we come to know God, and how we express our loyalty to God. The Methodist emphasis on "practical divinity" leads us to ask of all theological affirmations, "Does it ring true in my experience and in the experience of the Christian community?" If it does, experience has helped to validate the affirmation. If it is incompatible with our experience, the belief may either be a challenge to our experience or a challenge to the validity of the belief.

Experience, too, can be misleading and must be tested by Scripture, tradition, and reason. Feelings are not the final judge of authenticity. Without Scripture, tradition, and reason, faith is reduced to private, subjective feelings. God is easily made into a champion of selfish interests and a source of personal gratification. When feelings become more important than *being* and *doing*, discipleship is thwarted. Psychology verifies that self-interpretations of our experience can be gross distortions or reality. One's own personal experience needs the broader experience of others to inform, correct, and support it.

Reason as a Tool for Knowing God

Jesus said that the entire law is summed up in this commandment: " . . . you shall love the Lord your God with all your heart, and with all your soul, and with all your mind, and with all your strength" (Mark 12:30). The ability to reason is one of God's most precious gifts and a means of exploring, discerning, and sharing God's truth. *The Book of Discipline* contains the following statement:

> *Since all truth is from God, efforts to discern the connections between revelation and reason, faith and science, grace and nature, are useful endeavors in developing credible and communicable doctrine. We seek nothing less than a total view of reality that is decisively informed by the promises and imperatives of the Christian gospel.*[10]

John Wesley wrote the following reply in 1768 to a Cambridge professor who accused the Methodists of renouncing reason: "It is a fundamental principle with us that to renounce reason is to renounce religion; that religion and reason go hand and hand; and that all irrational religion is false religion."[11] Anti-intellectualism emerged among some Methodists on the American frontier; however, any attempt to denigrate reason must be resisted if United Methodists are to be true to their heritage and if they are to be a relevant voice in the contemporary world. Methodism's long tradition of involvement in higher education is testimony of the commitment to responsible stewardship of the mind.

Although an important tool for doctrine and theological exploration, reason has its limitations. Like all other gifts and resources made available for sharing God's life and mission, reason can be misdirected and abused. Without Scripture, tradition, and reason, faith is reduced to private, subjective feelings and God easily is made into the champion of selfish interests and a source of personal gratification. When feelings become more important than *being* and *doing*, discipleship is thwarted. Psychology verifies that self-interpretations of our experience can be gross distortions of reality. One's own personal experience needs the broader experience of others to inform, correct, and support it.

Scripture, tradition, reason, and experience provide Methodists with resources and guidelines for their endless journey into God's life and mission. When used as interrelated and mutually dependent tools, they enable persons of faith to grow in discipleship as they confront the challenges of living in the modern world. *The Book of Discipline* states, "These four sources—each making distinctive contributions, yet all finally working together—guide our quest as United Methodists for a vital and appropriate Christian witness."[12]

Conclusion

We live in a world that is increasingly indifferent or even hostile to Christian beliefs and practices. Even the most faithful disciples of Jesus Christ are challenged to rethink their faith in the face of changing concepts and demands. Living our faith in a personal God in an impersonal world and infinite universe is not easy. Trusting in the power of Transcendent Love in a society that relies on weapons of war, technological skill, and economic security presents us with a formidable challenge. A world filled with suffering, violence, poverty, and needless death raises questions about the existence of One who is both loving and powerful. Indeed, the journey of faith in the twenty-first century takes the faithful tthrough new theological territory.

Yet we are not left without resources in our journey. The God whom we follow into the future is present to guide, sustain, and shape us as individuals and a church. We enter the new territory with memory and hope. The historic doctrines of the Christian faith provide a framework within which we can explore the new territory. Through serious study of the Bible, the God who in Jesus Christ has made all things new continues to reveal the eternal and transcendent presence and purposes. From the tradition of the church in all its diversity, we are surrounded by a great cloud of witnesses who have followed the footsteps of God into new territory. Within the human mind and experience, the Holy Spirit is present to illumine, question, inform, and bring pardon and new life.

We, therefore, enter the future with confidence that the God who is sovereign of the past, present, and future will meet us in the challenges, dangers, uncertainties, and opportunities that await all faith pilgrims.

Opportunities for Reflection

The following questions may be used by groups wishing to discuss the material in Chapter Ten or by individuals wanting to reflect on issues raised within the chapter.

1. In this chapter, four tools–Scripture, tradition, reason and experience–are emphasized as reliable in engaging in theological reflection and maintaining sound doctrine. How do you make use of these tools ? Do you see them operating in your congregation? In other forums?

2. This chapter outlines six guidelines to follow in Bible study. Explore implications of each for your life. What are you currently doing? What do you want to do more of?

3. Wesley warned Methodists not to make *reason* an idol (page 81). What limitations might one find in the use of reason for theological reflection? How might one guard against possible limitations?

4. Historically, Methodists have emphasized *practical divinity.* Do you see this emphasis in current United Methodism? Why? Why not?

Chapter Eleven

A New Heaven and a New Earth

A local station televised a documentary on homeless people in Knoxville, Tennessee. One of those interviewed, "Chief," lived in a makeshift tent on the bank of the Tennessee River. Though homeless and addicted to alcohol, Chief was intelligent, sensitive, and compassionate. He could converse with University of Tennessee students and faculty about philosophy and politics as easily as he could discuss survival skills with street peers. He often visited the soup kitchen at the local United Methodist Church, where he engaged the pastors in theological discussions. The televised documentary closed with a camera shot of Chief, returning along the river to his crude shelter. Shaking his head from side to side, Chief was saying, "The world ain't supposed to be like this."

Needless suffering and premature death, violence and cruelty, economic and political exploitation, adverse poverty and environmental destruction ravage the earth. Sin and death, guilt and grief, loneliness and fear, anxiety and alienation continue to rob the human family of abundant life. Wars rage among nations. Racial and religious prejudices erupt into violent hatred, mocking the biblical vision of peace and the oneness of the human family. We know "the world ain't supposed to be like this."

John Wesley observed that "darkness, intellectual darkness, ignorance, with vice and misery attendant upon it, cover the earth!"[1] The pervasive evil in the world raised for Wesley a critical theological question: "But how astonishing is this, if there is a God in heaven! And if his eyes are over all the earth! Can he

despise the work of his own hand? . . . How is it possible to reconcile this with either the wisdom or goodness of God?"² The
only satisfactory explanation, according to Wesley, is that the
present condition of the world is not the final reality. God is
bringing a new heaven and a new earth. *The world is not what it
is going to be!*

Along with other Christians, United Methodists look toward
the consummation of God's purposes for all creation. *The Book
of Discipline* affirms, "We also look to the end time in which
God's work will be fulfilled. This prospect gives us hope in our
present actions, as individuals and as the Church. This expecta-
tion saves us from resignation and motivates our continuing witness and service."³ We are a people who live toward the coming
of God's new heaven and new earth.

The Future is Revealed in Jesus Christ

The Apostle Paul described Jesus Christ as "the image of
the invisible God, the firstborn of all creation . . . he is the beginning, the firstborn from the dead, so that he might come to have
first place in everything. For in him all the fullness of God was
pleased to dwell, and through him God was pleased to reconcile
to himself all things, whether on earth or in heaven . . ."
(Colossians 1:15,18-20). *In Jesus Christ the new heaven and new
earth is brought near; through Jesus Christ in the power of the
Holy Spirit, the reign of God's righteousness will be brought to
completion.*

The 'kingdom of God' is the central theme of Jesus' teaching. Mark's Gospel describes the beginning of Jesus' ministry in
these words: "Now after John was arrested, Jesus came to
Galilee, proclaiming the good news of God, and saying, 'The
time is fulfilled, and the kingdom of God has come near; repent
and believe in the good news.'" (Mark 1:14-15) In Jesus the
reign of God—the power, presence, and purposes of God—
comes near. Jesus Christ is the fulfillment of God's purposes. He
is the manifestation of God's power and presence. His teachings
point to the reign of God. His death and resurrection proclaim
the victory of God. His ascension affirms the promise of God.

In Jesus Christ, God manifests and inaugurates the new

heaven and new earth through the Word-Made-Flesh, Jesus Christ, "All things came into being . . . , and without him not one thing came into being" (John 1:3). From the very beginning, the Triune God has been conquering the powers of chaos, sin, and death, and establishing the reign of righteousness and love. As "the firstborn of the new creation," Jesus Christ makes visible God's creation—transforming past and anticipated future victory. Jesus Christ is the image of existence as God intends, the Savior/Redeemer of the old world, and the assurance of the final triumph of God's new world. Through the life, teachings, death, and resurrection of Jesus Christ, God's reign over creation and God's triumph over the powers of evil and death are brought near and secured. God's new heaven and new earth have begun and will be brought to completion.

God's future is forever breaking in upon the present as a sign and foretaste of God's ultimate triumph over chaos, sin, and death. Wherever the will of God is done, the kingdom of God is present. God's reign comes near whenever love triumphs over hate, justice reigns over injustice, the shackles of oppression and addiction are removed, reconciliation overcomes alienation, hope drives out despair, and wholeness and health are restored to creation. Everywhere Jesus went he brought love, forgiveness, hope, healing, insight, life, and judgment. His very presence judged those in whom hatred, vengeance, despair, injustice, oppression, sin and death reigned. Christ's invitation was and is, "Come. Let us live in a new world, the world of God's sovereignty over life and death." Live now in the light of God's victory.

God's Final Victory is Yet to Come

"Christ has died; Christ is risen; Christ will come again," we affirm in the Prayer of Great Thanksgiving.[4] The historic creeds of the church include belief in "the resurrection of the dead, and the life in the world to come" (The Nicene Creed), "the resurrection of the body and the life everlasting" (The Apostles' Creed), and "in the final triumph of righteousness and in life everlasting" (The Statement of Faith of the Korean Methodist Church).[5] From New Testament times to the present, the church has awaited the 'return of Christ,' or "the End.'

Eschatology–having to do with last things–has been a significant emphasis in the church's preaching and teachings.

As a youngster, I heard many sermons on "the end of time," "the Second Coming," and "the Final Judgment." Using the apocalyptic passages in the Bible (passages describing the End, including the books of Daniel and Revelation), preachers graphically portrayed the End of all things and the Second Coming of Christ, and the Final Judgment. They pointed to "signs" in the contemporary world that biblical prophecy was being fulfilled. Images of "weeping, wailing, and gnashing of teeth," "hellfire and brimstone," and the everlasting punishment of sinners summoned listeners to repent as the only appropriate preparation for the coming Judgment. I spent many sleepless nights afraid the end of the world would come "like a thief in the night." I feared I would be sent to hell, to burn forever. I was afraid that Christ would return and take my parents to heaven, leaving me to suffer tribulation and punishment.

Although the End or Second Coming (a term not used in the Bible) includes judgment upon and the destruction of evil, God's final victory brings hope, not despair. The Revelation to John, with its images of celestial conflict between God and the forces of evil, is supremely a book of hope and assurance rooted in God's triumph. It is the affirmation that the new heaven and new earth, inaugurated in Jesus Christ, will be brought to completion. Here is the writer's partial description of God's new creation:

Then I saw a new heaven and a new earth; for the first heaven and the first earth had passed away, and the sea was no more. And I saw the holy city, the new Jerusalem, coming down out of heaven from God, prepared as a bride adorned for her husband. And I heard a loud voice from the throne saying,

"See, the home of God is among mortals. He will dwell with them as their God; they will be his peoples, and God himself will be

with them;
he will wipe every tear from their eyes.
Death will be no more;
mourning and crying and pain will be no more,
for the first things have passed away."

And the one who was seated on the throne said,
"See, I am making all things new." Also, he
said, "Write this, for these words are trustwor-
thy and true." Then he said to me, "It is done! I
am the Alpha and the Omega, the beginning and
the end. To the thirsty I will give water as a gift
from the spring of the water of life. Those who
conquer will inherit these things, and I will be
their God and they will be my children."
(Revelation 21:1-8)

Belief in the Second Coming means that the victory begun in Jesus Christ will be brought to completion. God's purpose for the world will be fulfilled:

- Injustice will cease and justice will characterize all relationships;
- People will know themselves as beloved children of God, and will be valued for their identity as sons and daughters of God;
- Barriers among people will be removed;
- Righteousness and peace will prevail;
- The presence of God will cover the earth as waters cover the sea;
- Death, pain, and sorrow will pass away;
- The lowly will be exalted, the weak will be made strong;
- The kingdoms of this world will become the kingdom of Christ; and
- Christ shall reign forever!

John Wesley assured the early Methodists that God's reign will come to completion. To the poor and despised, the discouraged and defeated of his day, he proclaimed:

*. . . we have strong reason to hope that the work
he hath begun will carry on unto the day of his
Lord Jesus; that he will never intermit this
blessed work of his Spirit until he has fulfilled
all his promises; until he hath put a period to sin
and misery, and infirmity, and death; and re-
established universal holiness and happiness,
and caused all the inhabitants of the earth to
sing together, "Hallelujah! The Lord God
omnipotent reigneth!" Blessing, and glory, and
wisdom, and honour, and power, and might be
unto our Lord God forever and ever!*[6]

Today's United Methodists live toward God's final victory.
We believe that the salvation God has begun in us and all creation will be brought to completion. Through the work of the
Holy Spirit, we will be transformed into the likeness of Jesus
Christ and incorporated into Christ's reign over death and sin.
Although death brings grief and loss, we live with hope in life
eternal and in the assurance that "neither death, nor life, nor
angels, nor rulers, nor things present, nor things to come, nor
powers, nor height, nor depth, nor anything else in all creation,
will be able to separate us from the love of God in Christ Jesus
our Lord." (Romans 8:38-39)

God's Victory Includes All Creation

More than human life is to be transformed by God's final
victory. All creation will be healed, from the scarred majestic
mountains to the polluted flowing brook, from the depleted
ozone to the microscopic cell, from the diseased mighty oak to
the endangered spotted owl. The founder of Methodism captured
the pervasiveness of God's cosmic triumph in these words:

*He that sitteth upon the throne will soon change
the face of all things, and give a demonstrative
proof to all his creatures that "his mercy is over
all his works." The horrid state of things which
at present obtains will soon be at an end. On the*

*new earth no creature will kill or hurt or give
pain to any other. . . . Nay, no creature, no beast,
bird, or fish, will have any inclination to hurt
any other. For cruelty will be far away, and sav-
ageness and fierceness be forgotten. So that violence shall be heard no more, neither wasting or
destruction seen on the face of the earth. "The
wolf shall dwell with the lamb. . . and the leop-
ard shall lie down with the kid." "They shall not
hurt or destroy," from the rising of the sun to the
going down of the same.*[7]

God's Kingdom includes sovereignty over more than the
human spirit, and belief in God's final victory includes more
than confidence in personal life after death. Christ is sovereign
over all creation "and through him God was pleased to reconcile
to himself all things, whether on earth or in heaven . . ."
(Colossians 1:20). As Jesus calmed the stormy sea (Matthew
8:23-27), cast out demons (Mark 1:21-28), and raised Lazarus
from the dead (John 11:28-44), so the Risen and Ascended
Christ will heal all creation, conquer all demonic principalities
and powers, and bring new life to humanity.

Living Now Toward God's Final Victory

Christian discipleship is living *now* in the light of God's
final victory. We are called individually and as a church to live
today in terms of Christ's sovereignty over all creation. Belief in
life after death and in the consummation of God's purposes
revealed in Jesus Christ involves more than anticipation of the
future. It means living now as though God's new heaven and
new earth have been established, for in the Resurrection and
Ascension of Jesus Christ they have been assured.

Because of the new heaven and new earth brought in Jesus
Christ, we work for the healing of creation and justice for all
peoples. We live without barriers because we know that God has
reconciled all things and that all people are beloved children of
God. We shun violence and vengeance for we know the peace-
makers "will be called children of God" (Matthew 5:9) and

"those who are persecuted for righteousness' sake" know that "theirs is the kingdom of heaven." (Matthew 5:10) We face death and sorrow knowing that "death has been swallowed up in victory" (1 Corinthians 15:54), that God "will wipe every tear from their eyes" and "death will be no more; mourning and crying and pain will be no more, for the first things have passed away" (Revelation 21:4). We "strive first for the kingdom of God and his righteousness" (Matthew 6:33), for we know that God's Kingdom will come on earth as it is in heaven.

Since we believe that God will bring to completion what God began in Jesus Christ, we can live now with obedience born of hope and trust. Although evil, suffering, and death may continue to plague the earth, tempting us to disobedience and discouragement, we pursue Christlikeness with confidence and courage. We can look hatred and violence, injustice and exploitation, sin and death in the face and declare: *You cannot win! Your doom is sure!* In the words of Martin Luther:

> *And though this world, with devils filled, should*
> *   threaten to undo us,*
> *we will not fear, for God hath willed his truth to*
> *   triumph through us.*
> *The Prince of Darkness grim, we tremble not for*
> *   him;*
> *his rage we can endure, for lo, his doom is sure;*
> *one little word shall fell him.*
>
> *That word above all earthly powers, no thanks*
> *   to them, abideth;*
> *the Spirit and the gifts are ours, through him*
> *   who with us sideth.*
> *Let goods and kindred go, this mortal life also;*
> *the body they may kill; God's truth abideth still;*
> *his kingdom is forever.*[8]

Conclusion

Much in the world seems to contradict belief in God's victory over death and sin. Sin continues to pervade every dimension of life, and death's reality intrudes into every person's encounters. Disease, poverty, and violence regularly destroy millions of God's children. Creation itself is threatened by exploitation and abuse. As "Chief," the homeless man, said, "The world ain't supposed to be like this."

The good news is this: *One day, the world will not be like this!* Another world—a world transformed by the Eternal Word, made flesh in Jesus Christ—has come into being and triumphed. God's Kingdom is coming! In Jesus Christ a new world has dawned! God has begun a new heaven and a new earth. God will bring it to completion. We have been incorporated into Christ's death and resurrection. We faithfully and expectantly await the final victory. We are an Easter people who live now in the light of the coming dawn of God's eternal kingdom.

John Wesley's ministry spanned most of the eighteenth century. His last spoken words affirm the faith which had shaped his life. "The best of all is, God is with us."[9] As heirs of Wesley, United Methodists live the belief that God *has been* with us, God *is* with us, and God *shall* be with us! *Living that belief is the United Methodist way.*

Opportunities for Reflection

The following questions may be used by groups wishing to discuss the material in Chapter Eleven or by individuals wanting to reflect on issues raised within the chapter.

1. What do you believe about the End or the Second Coming? How do your beliefs affect how you feel about the future and how you live today?

2. Do you agree that God's saving and reconciling action in Jesus Christ includes all creation? What are the implications of such a belief for such issues as the environment, medicine, scientific and technological development, poverty, or international conflict?

3. In what ways do beliefs in life after death and God's ultimate victory over sin and death bring hope and courage? In what ways do such beliefs bring judgment?

Endnotes

Preface

[1] From "Thoughts upon Methodism," by John Wesley, in *The Works of John Wesley, Volume 9*: The Methodist Societies: History, Nature, and Design, edited by Rupert E. Davies (Abingdon Press, 1989); page 527.

Chapter 1

[1] From *The Life Experience and Gospel Labors of the Rt. Rev. Richard Allen*, by Richard Allen (Abingdon Press, 1983); page 30.

[2] From *The Life Experience and Gospel Labors of the Rt. Rev. Richard Allen*, by Richard Allen (Abingdon Press, 1983); page 30.

[3] From *The Book of Discipline of The United Methodist Church, 1992* (Copyright © 1992 by The United Methodist Publishing House), ¶65; pages 42-43.

[4] From *The Book of Discipline of The United Methodist Church, 1992* (Copyright © 1992 by The United Methodist Publishing House), ¶65; page 43.

[5] From *The Book of Discipline of The United Methodist Church, 1992* (Copyright © 1992 by The United Methodist Publishing House), ¶65; page 43.

[6] From *The Book of Discipline of The United Methodist Church, 1992* (Copyright © 1992 by The United Methodist Publishing House), ¶65; page 44.

[7] From *The Book of Discipline of The United Methodist Church, 1992* (Copyright © 1992 by The United Methodist Publishing House), ¶65; page 44.

[8] From *The Life Experience and Gospel Labors of the Rt. Rev. Richard Allen*, by Richard Allen (Abingdon Press, 1983); page 29.

Chapter 2

[1] From *The Book of Discipline of The United Methodist Church, 1992* (Copyright © 1992 by The United Methodist Publishing House), ¶ 66; page 49.

[2] From *The Book of Discipline of The United Methodist Church, 1992* (Copyright © 1992 by The United Methodist Publishing House), ¶ 66; pages 49-50.

[3] From *The Book of Discipline of The United Methodist Church, 1992* (Copyright © 1992 by The United Methodist Publishing House), ¶ 65; page 47.

[4] From "On Living without God" (Sermon 130), by John Wesley, in *The Works of John Wesley, Volume 4*: Sermons IV: 115-151, edited by Albert C. Outler (Abingdon Press, 1987); page 175.

[5] From "Journal: From February 1, 1737/38 to September 16, 1738," in *The Works of John Wesley, Volume 18*: Journals and Diaries I (1735-1738), edited by W. Reginald Ward and Richard Heitzenrater (Abingdon Press, 1988); page 228.

[6] From *The Source*, by James Michener (Random House, 1965); page 120.

[7] As cited in *Context for Discovery*, by Neal F. Fisher (Abingdon Press, 1981); page 17.

[8] From *Mein Kampf*, by Adolf Hitler (Houghton Mifflin Company, 1943); page 65. Emphasis original.

[9] From "On Living without God" (Sermon 130), by John Wesley, in *The Works of John Wesley, Volume 4*: Sermons IV: 115-151, edited by Albert C. Outler (Abingdon Press, 1987); page 171.

[10] From *Existentialism*, by Jean-Paul Sartre, translated by B. Frechtman (Philosophical Library, 1947); page 61.

[11] See *God the Economist: The Doctrine of God and Political Economy*, by M. Douglas Meeks (Fortress Press, 1989).

[12] From *Webster's New World College Dictionary*, third edition (Macmillan, 1996); s.v. hedonism, page 625.

[13] From "The Way to the Kingdom" (Sermon 7), by John Wesley, in *The Works of John Wesley, Volume 4: Sermons I: 1-33*, edited by Albert C. Outler (Abingdon Press, 1984); page 223.

[14] From "The Way to the Kingdom" (Sermon 7), by John Wesley, in *The Works of John Wesley, Volume 4: Sermons I: 1-33*, edited by Albert C. Outler (Abingdon Press, 1984); page 224.

[15] From *Not Every Spirit: A Dogmatics of Christian Disbelief*, by Christopher Morse (Trinity Press International, 1994); page 5.

[16] From "The Way to the Kingdom" (Sermon 7), by John Wesley, in *The Works of John Wesley, Volume 4: Sermons I: 1-33*, edited by Albert C. Outler (Abingdon Press, 1984); page 219.

[17] From "The Way to the Kingdom" (Sermon 7), by John Wesley, in *The Works of John Wesley, Volume 4: Sermons I: 1-33*, edited by Albert C. Outler (Abingdon Press, 1984); page 220.

[18] From "The Way to the Kingdom" (Sermon 7), by John Wesley, in *The Works of John Wesley, Volume 4: Sermons I: 1-33*, edited by Albert C. Outler (Abingdon Press, 1984); page 220ff.

Chapter 3

[1] From *Night*, by Elie Wiesel (Bantam Books, 1960); page 62.

[2] Alfred Tennyson, *"In Memoria."*

[3] From *The Book of Discipline of The United Methodist Church, 1992* (Copyright © 1992 by The United Methodist Publishing House) ¶65; page 42.

[4] From *The Book of Discipline of The United Methodist Church, 1992* (Copyright © 1992 by The United Methodist Publishing House) ¶65; page 42.

[5] From "Hark! the Herald Angels Sing," by Charles Wesley, in *The United Methodist Hymnal* (Copyright ©1989 by The United Methodist Publishing House); No. 240.

[6] From "A Service of Word and Table I, in *The United Methodist Hymnal* (Copyright © 1989 by The United Methodist Publishing House); page 9.

[7] From "A Modern Affirmation, in *The United Methodist Hymnal* (Copyright © 1989 by The United Methodist Publishing House); No. 885.

[8] From *Not Every Spirit: A Dogmatics of Christian Disbelief*, by Christopher Morse (Trinity Press International, 1994); page 180.

[9] From *Not Every Spirit: A Dogmatics of Christian Disbelief*, by Christopher Morse (Trinity Press International, 1994); page 181.

[10] "Holy Spirit, Come, Confirm Us," by Brian Foley. (Copyright © 1971 Faber Music, Limited.)

[11] From *The Book of Discipline of The United Methodist Church, 1992* (Copyright © 1992 by The United Methodist Publishing House) ¶67; pages 58-59.

[12] From *Letters and Paper from Prison*, by Dietrich Bonhoeffer, edited by Eberhard Bethge (Macmillan Company, 1953); page 361.

[13] From *Process and Reality: An Essay in Cosmology*, by Alfred North Whitehead, corrected edition, edited by David Ray Griffin and Donald W. Sherburne (Free Press, 1978); page 351.

[14] From *Wesley and the People Called Methodists*, by Richard P. Heitzenrater (Abingdon Press, 1995); page 308.

[15] From "I'll Praise My Maker While I've Breath," by Isaac Watts in *The United Methodist Hymnal* (Copyright ©1989 by The United Methodist Publishing House); No. 60.

Chapter 4

[1] From "A Caution against Bigotry" (Sermon 38), by John Wesley, in *The Works of John Wesley, Volume 2: Sermons II: 34-70*, edited by Albert C. Outler (Abingdon Press, 1985); page 76.

[2] From *Night*, by Elie Wiesel (Bantam Books, 1960); page 62.

[3] This insight comes primarily from Meeks in his book *God and the Economist: The Doctrine of God and Political Economy* (Fortress Press, 1989).

⁴ See "The Image of God" (Sermon 141), by John Wesley, in *The Works of John Wesley, Volume 4*: Sermons IV: 115-151, edited by Albert C. Outler (Abingdon Press, 1987); pages 292ff. Also, see "Toward a Wesleyan Social Ethic," by James C. Logan, in *Wesleyan Theology Today: A Bicentennial Theological Consultation*, edited by Theodore Runyan (Kingswood Books, 1985); page 365.

⁵ From "Salvation by Faith" (Sermon 1), by John Wesley, in *The Works of John Wesley, Volume 1*: Sermons I: 1-33, edited by Albert C. Outler (Abingdon Press, 1984); page 117.

⁶ From *Not Every Spirit: A Dogmatics of Christian Disbelief*, by Christopher Morse (Trinity Press International, 1994); page 265.

⁷ From "Have Thine Own Way, Lord," by Adelaide A. Pollard in *The United Methodist Hymnal*. (Copyright ©1989 by the United Methodist Publishing House); No. 382.

Chapter 5

¹ From *The Book of Discipline of The United Methodist Church, 1992* (Copyright © 1992 by The United Methodist Publishing House), ¶67; page 60.

² From *The Book of Discipline of The United Methodist Church, 1992* (Copyright © 1992 by The United Methodist Publishing House), ¶67; page 67.

³ From "The One Thing Needful" (Sermon 146), by John Wesley, in *The Works of John Wesley, Volume 4*: Sermons IV: 115-151, edited by Albert C. Outler (Abingdon Press, 1987); page 354.

⁴ From "The One Thing Needful" (Sermon 146), by John Wesley, in *The Works of John Wesley, Volume 4*: Sermons IV: 115-151, edited by Albert C. Outler (Abingdon Press, 1987); page 354.

⁵ From *The Book of Discipline of The United Methodist Church, 1992* (Copyright © 1992 by The United Methodist Publishing House), ¶67; page 60.

⁶ From *The Book of Discipline of The United Methodist Church, 1992* (Copyright © 1992 by The United Methodist Publishing House), ¶67; page 60. Used by permission.

⁷ From "Original Sin" (Sermon 44), by John Wesley, in *The Works of John Wesley, Volume 2*: Sermons II: 34-70, edited by Albert C. Outler (Abingdon Press, 1985); page 172.

⁸ From "Original Sin" (Sermon 44), by John Wesley, in *The Works of John Wesley, Volume 2*: Sermons II: 34-70, edited by Albert C. Outler (Abingdon Press, 1985); page 173.

⁹ From *Whatever Became of Sin?*, by Karl Menninger (Hawthorne Books, 1973).

¹⁰ *The New York Times*, January 8, 1992.

¹¹ From "Just as I Am, Without One Plea," by Charlotte Elliott, in *The United Methodist Hymnal*. (Copyright © 1989 by The United Methodist Publishing House); No. 357.

¹² From "Original Sin" (Sermon 44), by John Wesley, in *The Works of John Wesley, Volume 2*: Sermons II: 34-70, edited by Albert C. Outler (Abingdon Press, 1985); page 185.

Chapter 6

¹ From *The Book of Discipline of The United Methodist Church, 1992* (Copyright © 1992 by The United Methodist Publishing House), ¶65; page 42.

² From "The End of Christ's Coming" (Sermon 62), in *The Works of John Wesley, Volume 2*: Sermons II: 34-70, edited by Albert C. Outler (Abingdon Press, 1985); ages 482-83.

³ "Introduction," by Albert C. Outler, in *The Works of John Wesley, Volume 1*: Sermons I: 1-33, edited by Albert C. Outler (Abingdon Press, 1984); page 13.

⁴ From *The Book of Discipline of The United Methodist Church, 1992* (Copyright © 1992 by The United Methodist Publishing House), ¶65; page 44.

⁵ From *The Book of Discipline of The United Methodist Church, 1992* (Copyright © 1992 by The United Methodist Publishing House), ¶65; page 44.

⁶ From *The Book of Discipline of The United Methodist Church, 1992* (Copyright © 1992 by The United Methodist Publishing House), ¶65; page 44.

⁷ From *The Book of Discipline of The United Methodist Church, 1992* (Copyright © 1992 by The United Methodist Publishing House), ¶69; page 86.

[8] From "Salvation by Faith" (Sermon 1), by John Wesley, in *The Works of John Wesley, Volume 1*: Sermons I:33, edited by Albert C. Outler (Abingdon Press, 1984): pages 117-18.

[9] From *The Book of Discipline of The United Methodist Church, 1992* (Copyright © 1992 by The United Methodist Publishing House), ¶65; page 45.

[10] From "A Plain Account of the People Called Methodists, in a Letter to the Rev. Mr. Perronet, Vicar of Shoreham in Kent," by John Wesley, in *The Works of John Wesley, Volume 9*: The Methodist Societies: History, Nature, and Design, edited by Rupert E. Davies (Abingdon Press, 1989); pages 256-57.

[11] From "The Scripture Way of Salvation" (Sermon 43), in *The Works of John Wesley, Volume 2*: Sermons II: 34-70, edited by Albert C. Outler (Abingdon Press, 1985); page 157.

[12] From *The Book of Discipline of The United Methodist Church, 1992* (Copyright © 1992 by The United Methodist Publishing House), ¶65; page 45.

[13] From "Journal: From February 1, 1737/38 to September 16, 1738," by John Wesley, in *The Works of John Wesley, Volume 18*: Journal and Diaries I (1735-1738), edited by W. Reginald Ward and Richard P. Heitzenrater (Abingdon Press, 1988); pages 249-50.

[14] From *The Book of Discipline of The United Methodist Church, 1992* (Copyright © 1992 by The United Methodist Publishing House), ¶65; page 45.

[15] From *The Book of Discipline of The United Methodist Church, 1992* (Copyright © 1992 by The United Methodist Publishing House), ¶65; page 46.

[16] From *The Book of Discipline of The United Methodist Church, 1992* (Copyright © 1992 by The United Methodist Publishing House), ¶65; page 46.

[17] From "On Perfection" (Sermon 76), by John Wesley, in *The Works of John Wesley, Volume 3*: Sermons III: 71-114, edited by Albert C. Outler (Abingdon Press, 1986); page 74.

[18] From "Love Divine, All Love's Excelling," by Charles Wesley, in *The United Methodist Hymnal* (Copyright © 1989 by The United Methodist Publishing House); No. 384.

[19] From, "What is Methodism's Theological Contribution Today?", by Theodore Runyon, in *Wesleyan Theology Today, A Bicentennial Theological Consultation*, edited by Theodore Runyan (Kingswood Books, 1985); page 12.

[20] From "A Statement of Faith of the Korean Methodist Church," in *The United Methodist Hymnal* (Copyright © 1989 by The United Methodist Publishing House); No. 884.

Chapter 7

[1] This is the term Wesley often used to describe the Christian life and his own desire.

[2] From *The Book of Discipline of The United Methodist Church, 1992* (copyright © 1992 by The United Methodist Publishing House); ¶ 65; page 46.

[3] From *The Book of Discipline of The United Methodist Church, 1992* (copyright © 1992 by The United Methodist Publishing House); ¶ 65; page 47.

[4] Some Moravians believed that good works done prior to conversion were "splendid sins."

[5] From *The Book of Discipline of The United Methodist Church, 1992* (copyright © 1992 by The United Methodist Publishing House); ¶ 67; page 73.

[6] From "Journal: From February 1, 1737/38 to September 16, 1738," by John Wesley, in *The Works of John Wesley, Volume 18*: Journals and Diaries I (1735-1738), edited by W. Reginald Ward and Richard P. Heitzenrater (Abingdon Press, 1988); page 228.

[7] From *The Book of Discipline of The United Methodist Church, 1992* (copyright © 1992 by The United Methodist Publishing House); ¶ 67; pages 72-73.

[8] From *The Book of Discipline of The United Methodist Church, 1992* (copyright © 1992 by The United Methodist Publishing House); ¶ 67; page 73.

[9] From *The Book of Discipline of The United Methodist Church, 1992* (copyright © 1992 by The United Methodist Publishing House); ¶ 67; page 71.

[10] From *Wesley and the People Called Methodists*, by Richard P. Heitzenrater (Abingdon Press, 1995); page 199.

¹¹ From "Rules of the Band Societies, Drawn up Dec. 25, 1738," by John Wesley, in *The Works of John Wesley, Volume 9*: The Methodist Societies: History, Nature, and Design, edited by Rupert E. Davies (Abingdon Press, 1989); page 199.

¹² From *The Cost of Discipleship*, by Dietrich Bonhoeffer (Macmillan Company, 1959); pages 45ff.

¹³ From "Jesus, United by Thy Grace," by Charles Wesley, in *The United Methodist Hymnal* (Copyright © 1989 by The United Methodist Publishing House); No. 561.

¹⁴ From "A Covenant Prayer in the Wesleyan Tradition," in *The United Methodist Hymnal* (Copyright © 1989 by The United Methodist Publishing House); No. 607. This is a twentieth century adaptation of the prayer Wesley and the early Methodists used. This modern version may misconstrue the sense of costly discipleship by changing "exalted for thee, or trodden under foot for thee" to "brought low by thee."

Chapter 8

¹ From *The Book of Discipline of The United Methodist Church, 1992* (Copyright © 1992 by The United Methodist Publishing House); ¶ 67, page 69.

² From "Love Divine, All Loves Excelling," by Charles Wesley, in *The United Methodist Hymnal* (Copyright © 1989 by The United Methodist Publishing House); No. 384.

³ From *The Book of Discipline of The United Methodist Church, 1992* (Copyright © 1992 by The United Methodist Publishing House); ¶ 67, page 62.

⁴ From *The Book of Discipline of The United Methodist Church, 1992* (Copyright © 1992 by The United Methodist Publishing House); ¶ 67, page 67.

⁵ From *The Book of Discipline of The United Methodist Church, 1992* (Copyright © 1992 by The United Methodist Publishing House); ¶ 67, page 67.

⁶ From *The Book of Discipline of The United Methodist Church, 1992* (Copyright © 1992 by The United Methodist Publishing House); ¶ 67, page 67.

⁷ From "A Service of Word and Table I," in *The United Methodist Hymnal* (Copyright © 1989 by The United Methodist Publishing House); page 11.

⁸ From "A Service of Word and Table I," in *The United Methodist Hymnal* (Copyright © 1989 by The United Methodist Publishing House); page 7.

⁹ From "The Means of Grace" (Sermon 16), by John Wesley, in *The Works of John Wesley, Volume 1*: Sermons I: 1-33, edited by Albert C. Outler (Abingdon Press, 1984); page 384.

¹⁰ From *The Book of Discipline of The United Methodist Church, 1992* (Copyright © 1992 by The United Methodist Publishing House); ¶ 67, page 66.

¹¹ From "The Preface to Sermons on Several Occasions," by John Wesley, in *The Works of John Wesley, Volume 1*: Sermons I: 1-33, edited by Albert C. Outler (Abingdon Press, 1984); page 105.

¹² From "A Short History of the People Called Methodists," by John Wesley, in *The Works of John Wesley, Volume 9*: The Methodist Societies: History, Nature, and Design, edited by Rupert E. Davies (Abingdon Press, 1989); page 484.

Chapter 9

¹ From "Of the Church" (Sermon 74), by John Wesley, in *The Works of John Wesley, Volume 3*: Sermons III: 71-113, edited by Albert C. Outler (Abingdon Press, 1986); page 46.

² From *Biblical Perspectives on Evangelism*, by Walter Brueggemann (Abingdon Press, 1993); p. 90f.

³ From *The Book of Discipline of The United Methodist Church, 1992* (Copyright © 1992 by The United Methodist Church; ¶ 65, page 44.

⁴ From *The Book of Discipline of The United Methodist Church, 1992* (Copyright © 1992 by The United Methodist Publishing House); ¶67, pages 66-67.

⁵ From *The Book of Discipline of The United Methodist Church, 1992* (Copyright © 1992 by The United Methodist Publishing House); ¶69, page 85.

⁶ From "On God's Vineyard" (Sermon 107), by John Wesley, in *The Works of John Wesley, Volume 3*: Sermons III: 71-114, edited by Albert C. Outler (Abingdon Press, 1986); page 510.

7 From "Catholic Spirit" (Sermon 39), by John Wesley, in *The Works of John Wesley, Volume 2*: Sermons II: 34-70, edited by Albert C. Outler (Abingdon Press, 1985); pages 86-87.

8 From "Catholic Spirit" (Sermon 39), by John Wesley, in *The Works of John Wesley, Volume 2*: Sermons II: 34-70, edited by Albert C. Outler (Abingdon Press, 1985); page 93.

9 From "The Church of Christ, in Every Age," by Fred Pratt Green (©1971, Hope Publishing Co.).

Chapter 10

1 From *The Book of Discipline of The United Methodist Church, 1992* (Copyright © 1992 by The United Methodist Publishing House); ¶68, page 74.

2 From "Conciliar Theology: A Report" by Thomas A. Langford, in *Quarterly Review*, Summer 1989; page 9.

3 From "Conciliar Theology: A Report" by Thomas A. Langford, in *Quarterly Review*, Summer 1989; page 9.

4 From *The Book of Discipline of The United Methodist Church, 1992* (Copyright © 1992 by The United Methodist Publishing House); ¶67, page 59.

5 From *A Plain Account of Christian Perfection*, by John Wesley (Epworth Press, 1952); page 6.

6 From "Introduction," by Albert C. Outler, in *The Works of John Wesley, Volume 1*: Sermons I: 1-33, edited by Albert C. Outler (Abingdon Press, 1984); page 57.

7 From *The Book of Discipline of The United Methodist Church, 1992* (Copyright © 1992 by The United Methodist Publishing House); ¶68, page 79.

8 From "John Wesley and the Wholeness of Scripture," by Timothy L. Smith, in *Interpretation*, July 1985; page 250.

9 From *The Book of Discipline of The United Methodist Church, 1992* (Copyright © 1992 by The United Methodist Publishing House); ¶68, page 81.

10 From *The Book of Discipline of The United Methodist Church, 1992* (Copyright © 1992 by The United Methodist Publishing House); ¶68, page 82.

11 "A Letter to the Rev. Dr. Rutherford," by John Wesley, in *The Letters of the Rev. John Wesley, A.M.*, standard edition, edited by John Telford (Epworth Press, 1931), page 364.

12 From *The Book of Discipline of The United Methodist Church, 1992* (Copyright © 1992 by The United Methodist Publishing House); ¶68, page 82.

Chapter 11

1 From "The General Spread of the Gospel" (Sermon 63), by John Wesley, in *The Works of John Wesley, Volume 2*: Sermons II: 34-70, edited by Albert C. Outler (Abingdon, 1985); page 485.

2 From "The General Spread of the Gospel" (Sermon 63), by John Wesley, in *The Works of John Wesley, Volume 2*: Sermons II: 34-70, edited by Albert C. Outler (Abingdon, 1985); page 488.

3 From *The Book of Discipline of The United Methodist Church, 1992* (Copyright © 1992 by The United Methodist Publishing House, 1992), ¶65; p. 43.

4 From *The United Methodist Hymnal* (Copyright © 1989 by The United Methodist Publishing House); page 10.

5 From *The United Methodist Hymnal* (Copyright ©1989 by The United Methodist Publishing House); numbers 880, 881, and 884.

6 From "The General Spread of the Gospel (Sermon 63), by John Wesley, in *The Works of John Wesley, Volume 2*: Sermons II: 34-70, edited by Albert C. Outler (Abingdon Press, 1985); page 499.

7 From "The New Creation" (Sermon 64), by John Wesley, in *The Works of John Wesley, Volume 2*: Sermons II: 34-70, edited by Albert C. Outler (Abingdon Press, 1985); page 509.

8 From "A Mighty Fortress Is Our God," by Martin Luther, in *The United Methodist Hymnal* (Copyright © 1989 by The United Methodist Publishing House); no. 110.

9 From *Wesley and the People Called Methodists*, by Richard P. Heitzenrater (Abingdon, 1995); page 308.